T3-BNY-839

HAPPINESS
and
HARDSHIP

HAPPINESS
and
HARDSHIP

*Opportunity and Insecurity
in New Market Economies*

CAROL GRAHAM

STEFANO PETTINATO

BROOKINGS INSTITUTION PRESS
Washington, D.C.

Copyright © 2002
THE BROOKINGS INSTITUTION
1775 Massachusetts Avenue, N.W., Washington, D.C. 20036
www.brookings.edu

All rights reserved

Library of Congress Cataloging-in-Publication data

Graham, Carol, 1962–
  Happiness and hardship : opportunity and insecurity in new market
economies / Carol Graham and Stefano Pettinato.
    p.   cm.
Includes bibliographical references and index.
  ISBN 0-8157-0240-X (cloth : alk. paper) —
  ISBN 0-8157-0241-8 (pbk. : alk. paper)
  1. Income distribution—Psychological aspects.   2. Economic
development—Psychological aspects. 3. Happiness.   4. Income
distribution—Latin America—Psychological aspects.   I. Pettinato,
Stefano.   II. Title.
  HC79.I5 G684 2002
  338.9'001'9—dc21   2001006144

9 8 7 6 5 4 3 2 1

The paper used in this publication meets minimum requirements of the American
National Standard for Information Sciences—Permanence of Paper for
Printed Library Materials: ANSI Z39.48-1992.

Typeset in Minion

Composition by R. Lynn Rivenbark
Macon, Georgia

Printed by R. R. Donnelley and Sons
Harrisonburg, Virginia

338. 90019
G 738h

ß THE BROOKINGS INSTITUTION

The Brookings Institution is an independent organization devoted to nonpartisan research, education, and publication in economics, government, foreign policy, and the social sciences generally. Its principal purposes are to aid in the development of sound public policies and to promote public understanding of issues of national importance. The Institution was founded on December 8, 1927, to merge the activities of the Institute for Government Research, founded in 1916, the Institute of Economics, founded in 1922, and the Robert Brookings Graduate School of Economics and Government, founded in 1924. The Institution maintains a position of neutrality on issues of public policy to safeguard the intellectual freedom of the staff.

Board of Trustees
James A. Johnson
Chairman

Leonard Abramson
Michael H. Armacost
Elizabeth E. Bailey
Zoë Baird
Alan R. Batkin
James W. Cicconi
Alan M. Dachs
D. Ronald Daniel
Robert A. Day
Lawrence K. Fish
William C. Ford Jr.

Cyrus F. Freidheim Jr.
Bart Friedman
Stephen Friedman
Ann M. Fudge
Henry Louis Gates Jr.
Jeffrey W. Greenberg
Brian L. Greenspun
Lee H. Hamilton
William A. Haseltine
Teresa Heinz
Samuel Hellman
Joel Z. Hyatt
Shirley Ann Jackson
Robert L. Johnson

Ann Dibble Jordan
Michael H. Jordan
Marie L. Knowles
David O. Maxwell
Mario M. Morino
Steven Rattner
Rozanne L. Ridgway
Judith Rodin
Warren B. Rudman
Leonard D. Schaeffer
Joan E. Spero
John L. Thornton
Vincent J. Trosino
Stephen M. Wolf

Honorary Trustees
Rex J. Bates
Louis W. Cabot
A. W. Clausen
William T. Coleman Jr.
Lloyd N. Cutler
Bruce B. Dayton
Douglas Dillon
Charles W. Duncan Jr.
Walter Y. Elisha
Robert F. Erburu
Robert D. Haas
Andrew Heiskell
F. Warren Hellman
Robert A. Helman

Roy M. Huffington
Vernon E. Jordan Jr.
Breene M. Kerr
James T. Lynn
Jessica Tuchman Mathews
Donald F. McHenry
Robert S. McNamara
Mary Patterson McPherson
Arjay Miller
Constance Berry Newman
Maconda Brown O'Connor
Donald S. Perkins
Samuel Pisar

J. Woodward Redmond
Charles W. Robinson
James D. Robinson III
Howard D. Samuel
B. Francis Saul II
Ralph S. Saul
Henry B. Schacht
Michael P. Schulhof
Robert Brookings Smith
Morris Tanenbaum
John C. Whitehead
James D. Wolfensohn
Ezra K. Zilkha

To the roots of our happiness:

Carol's John and their three little A's

Stefano's Marla, and mother and father

Foreword

I t is an age-old puzzle why some societies seem to tolerate significant degrees of economic hardship and yet retain political and social stability, while others break into violent protest as a result of much smaller economic declines or shocks. This book attempts to shed light on these issues from a novel perspective: subjective well-being. Psychologists have analyzed subjective well-being, or happiness, in detail for decades. Yet only recently has it become the subject of economic analysis, which until now has concentrated on advanced industrialized economies. Carol Graham and Stefano Pettinato provide a new conceptual framework for analyzing the relationship between subjective well-being and the political sustainability of market-oriented economic growth in developing economies that are in the process of integrating into the world economy.

Several variables—such as marital status, employment, and inflation—are known to influence happiness. Graham and Pettinato have identified others that have important effects on how individuals perceive well-being: macroeconomic volatility, globalization of information, increasing income mobility, and inequality driven by technology-led growth.

The authors begin by explaining data and measurement problems involved in studying mobility and summarize general mobility trends in developing countries. They then provide new data on subjective well-being in seventeen Latin American countries and Russia. They find that the sociodemographic determinants of happiness, such as the effects of age and unemployment, are very similar to those in the United States and Europe. They also find that relative income differences have important effects on how individuals assess well-being, particularly when they are above the abject poverty line. Those in the middle or lower middle of the income distribution are more likely to be dissatisfied with their economic status than are the very poorest groups. Furthermore, volatility in income flows can have negative effects on perceived well-being, even among upwardly mobile individuals. The authors' survey research in Peru and Russia found that a majority of respondents with upward mobility gave negative assessments of their past economic progress. The frustrated respondents in the sample tend to be less supportive of market policies and of democracy than are non-frustrated respondents.

Further research is necessary to understand the implications of these frustrations for future economic and political behavior. Some studies suggest that excessive concern for relative income differences can lead to nonoptimal forms of economic behavior (such as conspicuous consumption to demonstrate wealth) and risky behavior (such as gambling to increase wealth at the margin). Particularly in low-income households, such behavior typically comes at the expense of savings or of investments in their children's education.

Graham and Pettinato identify a set of policies—ranging from improving education systems to more broad-based provision of safety nets and social insurance—to address some of the causes of the frustration or unhappiness that they find. These policies aim to increase mobility and provide new opportunities for low-income individuals, and possibly improve perceived, as well as actual, well-being. They also help protect individuals from income volatility and insecurity. Finally, the book points to the need for better understanding of the intersection between behaviorally driven frustrations and perceptions and those that can be influenced by policy. This will entail new kinds of data, as well as interdisciplinary research efforts that combine both economic and psychological approaches.

The authors wish to thank Henry Aaron, George Akerlof, Alan Angell, Eduardo Aninat, Ken Arrow, Barry Bosworth, Nancy Birdsall, David Blanchflower, Samuel Bowles, Gary Burtless, Christopher Carroll, Julio Cotler, Ed Diener, Bill Dickens, Steven Durlauf, Richard Easterlin, Josh

Epstein, Clifford Gaddy, George Graham, James Granato, Ross Hammond, Rachel Kranton, Michael Kremer, Marta Lagos, Martha Merritt, Gabriel Ortiz de Zevallos, Andrew Oswald, Karen Remmer, Jaime Saavedra, Isabel Sawhill, Charlie Schultze, John Steinbruner, Alois Stutzer, Nancy Truitt, Mariano Tommasi, Richard Webb, Kurt Weyland, Carol Wise, and Peyton Young for helpful comments on earlier drafts or at presentations of the research. They are also indebted to the research teams at the Latinobarometro in Santiago and the Instituto Cuanto in Peru, and to Barry Popkin at the University of North Carolina for assistance with the Russian survey research.

At Brookings, Robert Litan supported this project throughout. Kris McDevitt and Sun Kordel provided invaluable logistical assistance, and Linda Gianessi provided administrative oversight. Martha Gottron edited the manuscript and Catherine Theohary verified its factual content, Carlotta Ribar proofread the pages, and Mary Mortensen provided the index.

The authors are grateful to the John D. and Catherine T. MacArthur Foundation and to the Tinker Foundation for generous financial support of this project.

The views expressed in this volume are those of the authors and should not be ascribed to any person or institution acknowledged above or to the trustees, officers, or other staff members of the Brookings Institution.

MICHAEL H. ARMACOST
President

December 2001
Washington, D.C.

Contents

HAPPINESS
and
HARDSHIP

1

New Approaches to Old Inequities: Mobility, Opportunity, and Subjective Well-Being

This book explores a number of relationships that ultimately underlie the sustainability of market-based economic growth. An age-old puzzle is why some societies seem to tolerate significant degrees of economic hardship and yet retain political and social stability, whereas others break into violent protest in response to much smaller economic declines or shocks. A related puzzle is why some societies with high levels of income inequality, such as the United States and much of Latin America, broadly support market policies, while societies with much less inequality, such as some European and Eastern European countries, harshly criticize the market process in general and its distributive outcomes in particular.

We take the view that the political sustainability of market-oriented growth is as much determined by relative income levels and trends as by absolute ones and that opportunity and mobility over time are as important as current distributive outcomes. In addition, we posit that individuals' *subjective* assessments of their economic progress, as well as their expectations about the future, are as important as are objective trends in influencing their responses to economic incentives and their attitudes toward market policies.

Two concepts from the economics literature are central to this view and provide a conceptual frame for much of our analysis. These are the so-called tunnel effect, described in a classic 1973 article by Albert Hirschman, and the prospect of upward mobility, or POUM, hypothesis, most recently elaborated in a 1998 paper by Roland Benabou and Efe Ok.

Hirschman begins with the assumption that an individual's welfare depends on his present state of contentment (for which income is a proxy) as well as on his expected future contentment (or income). In certain circumstances—for example, early in a country's development path—individual A's perceived welfare, or utility, is enhanced by the advancements of individual B, because B's advancements supply positive information about what the future might be like for A. In an undefined short term, the positive effects on expectations override any feelings of envy A may experience. Yet if A does not eventually realize income gains or other advancements, then these expectations can turn into frustration. In this framework, Hirschman likened inequality during the growth process to a traffic jam in a tunnel. Initially those in a stalled lane gain hope from movements in other lanes. Yet if their lane never moves (persistent inequality), then that hope turns into frustration. The relevant point of reference, meanwhile, is the rate of change between the lanes of traffic (relative differences), not the types of cars that the individuals drive (absolute differences).[1]

A related concept is the POUM hypothesis. Many scholars have written about the effects that individuals' future expectations for themselves and their children have on their economic and political behavior.[2] Benabou and Ok offer an explicit hypothesis, positing that individuals who believe that they or their children have high prospects for upward mobility in the future are less likely to vote for redistribution in the present, because they do not want to vote for taxes that they or their children will have to pay in the future. Relying on U.S. data from the Panel Study on Income Dynamics (PSID) for 1969–76, they show how, over repeated periods, three-fourths of American families are poorer than average, yet two-thirds of American families expected future incomes above the mean and therefore do not support increased redistribution (higher tax rates).[3]

Both of these hypotheses hinge on individuals' *perceptions* about relative income differences and about future income change or mobility. As we

1. Hirschman (1973, pp. 544–66).
2. See, for example, Birdsall, Pinckney, and Sabot (1999); Nelson (1976), Perlman (1976); and Picketty (1995).
3. Benabou and Ok (1998).

show throughout this book, much of the behavior that we observe in our empirical work is driven by perceptions about future opportunities and their potential—or lack thereof—to reduce relative income differences, rather than by absolute levels of income or poverty.

Our approach is inspired in part by several recent studies that attempt to evaluate individuals' subjective well-being, or, broadly speaking, "happiness."[4] The results suggest that economists should revisit the standard assumptions about the role of rational, material self-interest in determining economic behavior. Although behavioral economists and psychologists have questioned these assumptions for years, mainstream economists and political scientists have been much more reluctant to do so.[5] The happiness studies, which concentrate primarily on the developed economies, find little correlation between country-level economic growth rates and mean levels of subjective well-being. In other words, they find no evidence that happiness increases as societies grow wealthier or that wealthier societies are happier than poorer ones (above a certain absolute minimum level of income), even though, on average, the wealthy are happier than the poor within individual societies.[6]

The effects of wealth on people's happiness within developed economies, meanwhile, are far less important than those of other factors

4. Most of these studies use the term "happiness" interchangeably with the more cumbersome term "subjective well-being," accepting that the former has dimensions that go well beyond the economic ones considered by this literature. For an excellent review of these definitions and the literature, see Easterlin (2000). For a review from the behavioral sciences perspective, see Diener and Biswas-Diener (1999).

5. For a review of the debate between mainstream economists and behavioral economists, see Roger Lowenstein, "Exuberance Is Rational," *New York Times Magazine,* February 11, 2001, p. 68; and Louis Uchitelle, "Chasing the Money but Also the Mind," *New York Times,* February 11, 2001, Sec. 3, p. 1. For a discussion of the impact of the results of the happiness work on the debate on taxes and employment in the developed economies, see Paul Krugman, "Pursuing Happiness," *New York Times,* March 29, 2000, p. A25.

6. In the United States real per capita income has more than doubled since World War II. The average reported level of happiness, however, is the same as it was in the late 1940s; the story is similar for Europe. Even in Japan, which had a fivefold increase in income per capita in the three decades since the 1950s, there was no change in average happiness levels; see Easterlin 2000. Blanchflower and Oswald (1999) find that average happiness levels decreased slightly from the 1970s to the 1990s in the United States and remained flat in the United Kingdom. Inglehart (1988) posits that the income level at which relative differences begin to matter more than absolute ones (at the country level) is $10,000 per capita. Our own findings suggest that the income level may be even lower.

such as employment, health, marriage, and age.[7] Macroeconomic variables other than income growth, such as inflation, unemployment, and macro-economic volatility, seem to have strong effects on happiness.[8] According to one study, in the United States and most countries in Europe—including those where unemployment benefits are very generous—being unemployed is equivalent in what the authors call "life dissatisfaction units" to dropping from the top to the bottom income quartile.[9] Our own analysis of region-wide data for Latin America finds that, controlling for a number of sociode-mographic variables, concerns about both inflation and unemployment have negative effects on happiness (discussed in detail in chapter 4).[10]

These findings by no means discount the tremendous importance of eco-nomic growth as a necessary condition for achieving a wide range of fun-damental societal objectives, including economic development, enhanced social welfare, and the reduction of poverty.[11] Yet they do suggest that fac-tors other than income growth affect individuals' assessments of their own welfare and that these same factors may also influence individuals'

7. In the United States and Europe, the following personal characteristics are positively and significantly associated with happiness: being employed, female, young or old (not middle age), educated, married, with few children, or belonging to a high-income quartile; see Blanchflower and Oswald (1999). Relying on cross-section data for the United States and Europe over several decades, they find that the relationship between age and happiness is U-shaped, turning upward at around age 40. Using cross-section data for Latin America for several years, Graham and Pettinato (2001) obtain a similar finding, with the turning point at age 46. Easterlin (2001), however, relying on synthetic cohorts constructed from the U.S. General Social Survey from 1972 to 1998, finds that age and happiness have a flat relationship.

8. The level of inflation "acceptable" to the public varies according to a country's past tra-jectory, as well as the extent to which there is indexation.

9. Blanchflower and Oswald (1999). For the macroeconomics of happiness in the United States and United Kingdom, see Di Tella, MacCulloch, and Oswald (1997).

10. These findings are based on responses to the 1999 Latinobarometro survey of more than 17,000 respondents in Latin America. See Graham and Pettinato (2001).

11. Economists generally agree that growth is necessary, if not always sufficient, for poverty reduction. See, for example, World Bank (2000). And increasingly economists ques-tion the validity—or at least the broad applicability across countries and time—of Kuznet's hypothesis that growth must initially lead to higher levels of inequality. See, for example, Barro (1999); Birdsall, Ross, and Sabot (1995); and Milanovic (1998). Market-oriented macroeconomic policies and open trading regimes seem to be a basic requirement for achiev-ing sustained growth, although there is less agreement on how to sustain such frameworks and manage exogenous shocks and volatility. See, among others, Rodrik (1999); Sachs and Warner (1995).

responses to economic incentives and policies.[12] Economists have tradi-tionally measured preferences by looking at behavior (revealed preferences). The use of survey data on subjective well-being or happiness is a relatively new approach that some economists are now using to determine how macroeconomic and microeconomic variables affect individual preferences. Although not without flaws, the approach has the potential to contribute to the understanding of seemingly "nonrational" economic behavior.[13]

For example, under certain circumstances, individuals' concern for rela-tive income differences can lead them to opt for conspicuous consump-tion—rather than making more "rational" investments in things such as their children's education—to demonstrate wealth status. Alternatively, such concerns can motivate risky behavior, such as gambling, to enhance status through wealth gains at the margin.[14] The role of relative income dif-ferences and of nonincome determinants of economic behavior is not yet fully understood, but it could have important implications for the future direction of market economies.

So far research on happiness has focused on developed economies largely because of the better availability of adequate data, particularly panel data. Yet some of the factors that influence individual assessments of well-being, such as income mobility, macroeconomic volatility, and occupational sta-tus, fluctuate more in developing countries and no doubt have implications for the happiness of individuals within those countries. Not surprisingly,

---

12. Pigou (1920) wrote that economic welfare, which could be measured with money, was only one component of welfare and that the elements of this component were largely deter-mined by the capacity to measure them.

13. For detail on the construction of welfare functions with this approach, see Frey and Stutzer (1999).

14. Veblen (1967) argued that in affluent societies, spending increasingly becomes a means to achieve social status rather than to meet needs. Cole, Mailath, and Postlewaite (1995) model how concern for relative wealth can generate conspicuous consumption when wealth is not directly observable. Arie Kapteyn (2000), in empirical work in the Netherlands, finds that, controlling for other variables, having wealthier friends and neighbors negatively affects savings. Hojman (2000) develops a model of consumption driven by inequality in Chile, where wealthier groups engage in conspicuous consumption and poor households make nonoptimal consumption decisions at the expense of long-term human capital investments. Robson (1992) develops a model of utility that is concave in wealth itself, but convex at some range when the indirect effects of status are included. Schor (1998) notes that Americans' debt service as a share of disposable income increased during the late 1980s and early 1990s along with a major consumption boom.

capturing these dynamics presents a number of measurement challenges, some but not all of which we have been able to overcome. Our objective in this book is to provide a new conceptual framework for analyzing the relationship between subjective well-being and objective economic trends in an increasingly integrated global economy as well as to provide some detailed empirical evidence from the emerging market economies.

We suggest that the way individuals perceive their well-being depends not only on already identified individual and within-country variables that influence happiness, such as marital status, employment, and inflation, but also on several variables related to international economic integration. These include macroeconomic volatility driven by contagion effects in external capital markets, the globalization of information, increasing income mobility (both upward and downward), and inequality driven by technology-led growth. Some of these trends, such as vulnerability to external capital flows, are directly related to integration in the international economy. Others, such as changes in income mobility and income distribution, are caused by the market reforms and liberalization of trade regimes that are a prerequisite for developing countries embarking on the process of integration.[15] Many authors have analyzed the causes and effects of these various trends.[16] This book focuses on how these trends affect perceived well-being. While a discussion of the causes of each of these trends is beyond our focus, their links, both direct and indirect, to the increased integration of the world economy and to the related increased flow of information across borders are pertinent to our analysis.

The effects of these variables may be stronger in developing economies in the process of integrating more fully into the international economy—with the consequent effects on income distribution and social mobility—than they are in the advanced industrial economies.[17] Perceptions of well-being in turn influence individuals' responses to economic incentives and their attitudes about the market. Unhappiness in such contexts may thus have

---

15. We thank one of our external readers for highlighting the need to distinguish between trends that are caused by international economic integration and those that are indirectly related or merely exacerbated by it.

16. Some of this literature is reviewed in chapter 3.

17. For a conceptual framework and initial exploration of the possible effects of globalization on economic and social mobility, see Birdsall and Graham (2000).

implications for the political sustainability of market reforms and for social stability more generally.

A Proposed Conceptual Framework

Psychologists have been analyzing subjective well-being, or happiness, in detail for decades. Yet only recently has it become the subject of economic analysis, and until now that analysis has been conducted primarily in the advanced industrial economies. Mobility, meanwhile, for the most part has been analyzed by sociologists rather than economists—although with some notable exceptions—and that analysis has also concentrated on the developed economies. In this book we build from the existing literatures on happiness and mobility and explore the links between subjective well-being and actual trends in mobility in several countries where market economies are emerging.

We first explain the data and measurement problems involved in studying mobility and then provide a summary of general trends in the developing countries based on the limited data available. We next explore the effects of the usual sociodemographic variables, such as age, gender, education, occupation, and marital status, on subjective well-being in the emerging market countries for which we have data (seventeen Latin American countries and Russia) and compare our results with similar analysis for the United States. We find that the sociodemographic determinants of subjective well-being in these studies are remarkably similar.

Starting with these "baseline" trends in mobility and happiness in emerging markets, we analyze the relationship between objective economic conditions and perceived well-being in Latin America, with comparative reference to Russia. We also explore the links between our results and attitudes about market policies and democracy. In a separate chapter, we undertake a detailed analysis of mobility and subjective well-being based on survey research and panel data from Peru and Russia.

Our analysis is framed by a set of contextual variables that we believe are particularly critical in the emerging market economies:

—The effects of market reforms on the mobility and opportunity of various age, income, and education cohorts;

—Relative income differences and their differential effects on the middle stratum, compared with the poor; and

—Macroeconomic volatility and related public concerns about vulnerability and insecurity.

First, we believe that poverty and inequality must be analyzed dynamically. We therefore focus on the effects of market reforms and globalization on trends in mobility and opportunity. The limited evidence suggests that the introduction of market policies—and the elimination of distortions that block the productive potential of the poor—can increase mobility and provide new opportunities for low-income people to move up the income ladder.[18]

Yet at the same time, the turn to the market and the widening differential in the rewards to skilled and unskilled labor also create new vulnerabilities—for those in the middle of the income spectrum as well as for the poor. Those vulnerabilities result in heightened public concerns about economic insecurity and about the wide and growing gaps between the winners and losers in the process. Our analysis in subsequent chapters shows how these concerns influence the subjective well-being of individuals in emerging market economies, even when they are faring relatively well in objective economic terms.

Second, and related to these trends, relative income differences have important effects on how individuals assess their well-being or "happiness." We posit that absolute income levels do matter, but that how much they matter is inversely related to their level; for example, the lower the level of per capita income in a country, the more absolute incomes matters to subjective assessments of well-being. Thus after crossing a certain minimum level of income (which varies across countries, time, and individuals), even upwardly mobile people may be dissatisfied if those around them are moving up more quickly (the tunnel effect) or if large gaps persist between them and the highest income groups. Those in the middle or lower middle of the income distribution are more likely to be dissatisfied than are the very poorest groups.

Our detailed survey research finds that, rather surprisingly, it is the most upwardly mobile people who are most negative in their self-assessments. Individuals in this group—the group we call "frustrated achievers"—are less positive about their future economic prospects and are less supportive

---

18. For a detailed description of such distortions and for how the turn to the market can eliminate such distortions, see Birdsall, Graham, and Sabot (1998).

of market policies than are those individuals who assess their situation positively.[19] Thus the frustrations of the upwardly mobile, beyond having obvious effects on individuals' happiness, may have implications for aggregate patterns of economic and political behavior. Our regionwide analysis supports this proposition, as we find evidence of a virtuous circle linking positive assessments of well-being, support for market policies, and support for democracy.

Third, we posit that the level of macroeconomic volatility in a country affects individuals' subjective well-being. As a result individuals place very different weights on the importance of job security, income, and social insurance policies when they are asked to assess the macroeconomic and political regimes under which they live. And as in the case of relative income differences, these issues tend to have more salience for those in the lower-middle and middle portions of the distribution than for those at the very bottom. Our regional data show that both inflation (the country level rate) and unemployment (individual status) have negative effects on reported well-being, or happiness. (This is discussed in detail in chapter 4; regression results are in table 4-3). Our more detailed survey data suggest that more volatility in income flows, even for the upwardly mobile, can have negative effects on perceived well-being.[20]

How recent the collective memory of volatility is—for example, the timing of reform—also seems to affect the importance that individuals attach to macroeconomic stability and economic growth compared with redistribution and social insurance issues, and in turn the influence that these trends and policies have on perceived well-being. Citizens in countries that have only recently stabilized are more supportive of market policies such as privatization, and less in favor of redistribution, than are citizens in countries where reforms are more established. This finding suggests that in volatile economic situations, citizens place a premium on growth and stability and turn their attention to distribution issues only later as reforms are consolidated. Like Hirschman, we posit that initial inequality, which is often viewed as an initial sign of economic progress, causes much less frustration than inequality that persists over time.

19. This finding was for the subset of frustrated achievers from Russia for which we had data about attitudes toward the market.
20. Income volatility, as measured by the coefficient of variation, was significantly higher for our frustrated achievers in Russia than it was for the rest of the sample.

A final and additional issue is the relationship between "social capital" and mobility. Although we explore this issue in much less detail than the others, we nonetheless posit that the different objectives underlying civic participation can result in social capital having very different effects on individual mobility rates, on perceived well-being, and on aggregate growth. This view is quite distinct from that taken by Putnam and others, which highlights the contributions that social capital makes to growth.[21] We distinguish between civic participation that is driven by economic necessity, such as soup kitchens or group credit schemes in poor countries, and voluntary participation in civic organizations, such as Putnam's famous choral groups.[22] The former play an important safety net role, but they can also be poverty traps, as risk-averse people may be afraid to leave the security provided by group membership (such as meals for the family from a soup kitchen) in order to seek better opportunities.[23]

Our analysis of data from Peru finds no link between upward mobility and participation in civic associations. When we distinguish between kinds of organizations and the reasons underlying participation, we find a link between upward mobility and participation in associations for noneconomic reasons. In contrast, there is no link between mobility and participation in associations for reasons of economic necessity. Our upwardly mobile respondents are less likely to be involved in group insurance or other joint economic schemes than are respondents whose mobility is not changing or is moving downward, and the upwardly mobile are more likely to seek acquaintances and new contacts outside their immediate reference group. They are also more likely to compare themselves with those outside their reference group as they assess their well-being.

Our analysis is not restricted to these issues, but they provide an analytical framework for our exploration of the relationship among inequality, opportunity, and public perceptions of those opportunities.

21. Putnam (1993). See also Knack and Keefer (1997).
22. The distinction that Granovetter (1973) makes between strong and weak ties in determining individual mobility rates is also relevant here and is discussed in detail later in the book.
23. For detail on the safety net role that these groups can play, see Graham (1994). For these groups as poverty traps, see Hoff (1996).

Contents of the Book

Chapter 2 briefly reviews the relevant literatures on happiness and on mobility and voting behavior. This review both provides a conceptual frame for some of the questions that we pose, yet also reveals the extent to which they have yet to be addressed by existing studies. Chapter 3 offers a conceptual framework for thinking about mobility and discusses some of the measurement challenges involved. It then reports on the limited evidence available on mobility and vulnerability in the emerging market countries. It also discusses two related trends: top-driven inequality and middle-income stress. We first introduced these trends, as well as new ways of measuring them, in recent work with Nancy Birdsall. We review that discussion here because of its relevance to our analysis of the relationship between objective mobility trends and individuals' subjective assessments of their well-being.[24]

Chapter 4 turns to the relationship between individual assessments of subjective well-being and macro-level variables such as inflation and unemployment. We relate our findings to individual attitudes about market reforms and about democracy. We used new data for Latin America, analyzing the relevant questions in a regionwide survey of public support for market reforms and for democratic institutions in seventeen countries in 1997, 1998, and 2000. At our request, the survey also included respondents' evaluations of their past progress, their expectations for the future, and a number of questions about how they compared themselves to others in a variety of reference groups. For a subset of these questions, we provide comparative evidence from Russia and the United States, relying on a panel survey, the RLMS, for the former, and a nonpanel survey, the General Social Survey, for the latter.

Chapter 5 reports the results of a detailed survey of mobility and subjective well-being that we developed and implemented in Peru. Our survey entailed repeated interviews of a subset of households from a 1991–2000 nationally representative panel. The survey also included several questions pertaining to the relationship between mobility and social capital. We then

---

24. Birdsall, Graham, and Pettinato (2000).

compare those results with some comparable, although less detailed, data from Russia. In the concluding chapter we discuss the implications of our findings for the design of economic and social policies in a globalized economy characterized by new opportunities and new vulnerabilities. We also pose several questions that our findings raise for future research.

2

Mobility, Subjective Well-Being, and Public Perceptions: Stuck in the Tunnel or Moving Up the Ladder?

Central to any exploration of the political economy of mobility is whether people are willing to accept more inequality (or the persistence of high levels of inequality) if economic change generates more opportunities and thus more mobility, including downward mobility.[1] One plausible explanation for voters' continued endorsement of market reforms in many emerging market countries despite the persistence or increase of inequality is that reforms create new opportunities and expectations of future upward mobility. Voters may perceive that market signals reward hard work, productivity, and innovation more than previously state-dominated economies did, thus making the move to the market acceptable in regions of high and increasing inequality such as Latin America and in regions of visible and painful downward mobility such as in Eastern Europe and the former Soviet Union. In Hirschman's terms, reforms give voters hope, at least initially, that they will get out of the tunnel traffic, even if progress is uneven in the early stages.

Yet that is an optimistic interpretation. Perhaps increased inequality and insecurity reflect deep and persistent differences across individuals and

1. For a definition of mobility, which includes absolute and relative mobility, time-dependence, positional, share, and directional income movement, see Fields (2000).

households in their capacity to exploit markets or in their access to education, employment, or property rights—leaving them permanently stuck in the tunnel, so to speak.[2] If inequality reflects discrimination against certain groups and historical handicaps that ensure the intergenerational transmission of poverty, then mobility, measured over lifetimes and even generations, will be low. Current acceptance of market reform could be the short-run outcome of the limited political voice of those excluded from new opportunities.

Which of these interpretations is correct? The existing political economy literature does not provide answers. Much of the literature has focused on the variables explaining the adoption and implementation of market reforms, and only recently has some work focused on the factors that make reforms politically sustainable among broad sectors of the population.[3] Most analysis is of an ex post nature; that is, it examines how populations vote in the period after reforms have been implemented.[4] We provide a new conceptual framework and new empirical evidence with which to analyze the political economy of mobility and market reforms.

Our analysis also relies on a host of other literatures as a point of departure. Mobility work, for example, traditionally has been the realm of sociologists, and no broad body of economics or political science literature covers mobility issues. Economists have certainly published some important works on the topic, but they focus primarily on the United States and on macro- and microeconomic determinants of mobility, rather than on political economy.[5] There is a wide body of literature covering the political economy of market reforms that, at least until now, has focused on inequality issues in a static manner, rather than on the dynamics of mobility, opportunity, and political behavior.[6] This book is part of a broader collaborative

2. Sen's (1995) classic definition of poverty, for example, centers on people's capabilities to participate as productive members of society, rather than just on their level of income.

3. See Graham (1998).

4. An excellent analysis of voting during reform episodes is in Stokes (1996). See also Weyland (1998).

5. For trends in the United States, see, for example, McMurrer and Sawhill (1998). Deaton and Paxson (1994) compare intergenerational mobility trends in the United States and Taiwan. For conceptual and methodological frameworks for measuring mobility, see Fields (2000) and Behrman (2000). For detailed research on U.S. intergenerational mobility, see Solon (1992).

6. See, among others, Geddes (1995); Graham (1998); Haggard and Webb (1994); Rodrik (1996).

effort to build from these existing literatures and to establish a new line of research on the economics and political economy of mobility in new market economies.[7]

To understand what underlies current patterns of economic and political behavior in the context of market reforms—and the extent to which these patterns are lasting—we believe that it is necessary to understand two phenomena about which there is limited information. The first is objective trends in mobility during reform: who is moving up, who is moving down, and why. Recent work has attempted to collect what information there is on mobility in the emerging market countries; that work is briefly reviewed in chapter 3. The second phenomenon is how people *perceive* their past mobility and their prospects of upward mobility in the future. This is clearly the most uncharted territory, which we explore in detail in the remaining chapters of the book.

Three bodies of literature inform our effort. The first attempts to measure overall economic well-being or happiness. This effort was pioneered by Richard Easterlin, and has been substantially expanded in recent years by economists such as Andrew Oswald, David Blanchflower, Bruno Frey, and Alois Stutzer, as well as by psychologists such as Ed Diener, Daniel Kahneman, and Amos Tversky.[8] The second is the political economy literature that focuses on the POUM hypothesis and examines the extent to which people's evaluations of their prospects of upward mobility determine their voting stance on redistribution issues.[9] Although this literature has dealt primarily with the developed economies, it nonetheless provides a useful framework for analyzing the political economy of mobility in the developing economies.

The third body of literature that informs our effort considers the role of networks, community organizations, and other forms of organization in determining people's mobility. These issues are often bundled into the catchall concept of "social capital," particularly since publication in 1993 of Robert Putnam's influential work, *Making Democracy Work*. While not discounting the importance of the work that Putnam inspired, we find the

---

7. The genesis of this effort—and the contribution of several scholars—is described in Birdsall and Graham (2000).

8. See, among others, Alesina, Di Tella, and MacCulloch (2000); Blanchflower and Oswald (1999); Diener (1984); Easterlin (1974); Frey and Stutzer (1999, 2000); Kahneman and Tversky (2000).

9. See Benabou and Ok (1998).

work of sociologist Mark Granovetter more relevant to our analysis.[10] We do not attempt an exhaustive review of these literatures but instead highlight work that has helped us in framing our thinking.

Happiness

The study of happiness, or subjective well-being, is a fairly new area for economists, although psychologists have been studying it for years. Some of the earliest economists, such as Jeremy Bentham, were concerned with the pursuit of individual happiness. As the field became more rigorous and quantitative, however, much narrower definitions of individual welfare, or utility, became the norm. In addition, economists have traditionally shied away from the use of survey data because of justifiable concerns that answers to surveys of individual preferences—and reported well-being—are subject to bias from factors such as the respondents' mood at the time of the survey and minor changes in the phrasing of survey questions, which can produce large skews in results.[11] Thus traditional economic analysis focuses on actual behavior, such as revealed preferences in consumption, savings, and labor market participation, under the assumption that individuals rationally process all the information at their disposal to maximize their utility.

In recent years, however, the strictly rational vision of economic decisionmaking has come under increasing scrutiny. One important innovation is the concept of bounded rationality, in which individuals are assumed to have access to limited or local information and to make decisions according to simple heuristic rules rather than complex optimization calculations.[12] A more recent trend, meanwhile, has been the increased influence of behavioral economics, which supplements the methods and research questions of economists with those more common to psychologists.

Daniel McFadden, for example, uses evidence from behavioral experiments to explain a great deal of seemingly nonrational behavior in economic decisionmaking.[13] Some such behavior results from perception

---

10. Granovetter (1973).
11. For a summary of the critiques of the use of survey data, see Bertrand and Mullainathan (2001).
12. See, among others, Conlisk (1996); Simon (1978).
13. McFadden (forthcoming). See also Kahneman and Tversky (2000).

errors arising from problems in the way information is stored, presented, and processed—for example, when equivalent lotteries, presented differently, are weighed differently by the same individuals, or when initial and easily experienced events, which are the most easily recalled, have disproportionate influence on economic decisions. Other seemingly nonrational behavior results from processes that lead individuals to make choices that are inconsistent with rationality narrowly defined—for example, when norms or rules lead to behavior guided by principles and exemplars rather than utilitarian calculus (a practice that most philosophers, if not economists, would welcome), or when judgments are influenced by the need or desire to project a self-image.

Particularly under these kinds of circumstances, survey data can contribute to understanding the decisionmaking process and its outcomes. Charles Manski, for example, has suggested that economics could benefit from more extensive usage of survey data. To test the predictive value of survey responses, he studied the relationship between stated intentions and subsequent behavior. His analysis is restricted to the simplest kind of intentions questions, those that call for "yes" or "no" answers, such as one posed to female respondents in a U.S. Census survey: "Looking ahead, do you expect to have any (more) children?" He finds that responses to intentions questions can be used to determine the best-case probabilities (within certain bounds) of respondents' future behavior.[14] Although most critics of such data assert that individuals are poor predictors of their futures, Manski finds that most of the divergences between intentions and actual behavior are attributable to the dependence of behavior on events not yet realized at the time of the survey, events that respondents could obviously not account for when formulating their answers. Unlike intentions questions, happiness questions do not require respondents to predict future behavior and therefore do not suffer from the divergences that result from unknown events.

Economists who work in the area broadly define happiness or subjective well-being as satisfaction with life in general (the three sets of terms are used interchangeably in most studies). Most studies of happiness are based on a very simple set of survey questions that typically ask respondents "How satisfied are you with your life" or "How happy are you with your life." Answers to this open-ended question obviously incorporate psychological

14. See, for example, Manski (1990); Dominitz and Manski (1996).

as well as material and sociodemographic factors. Critics used to defining welfare or utility in material or income terms bemoan the lack of precise definition in these questions. Yet the economists who use these surveys emphasize their advantages in making comparisons across cohorts of individuals—in which they find a surprising consistency in the patterns of responses both within and across countries—rather than in evaluating the actual happiness levels of specific individuals. Psychologists, meanwhile, find a significant degree of "validation" in subjective well-being surveys, wherein individuals who report higher levels of happiness actually smile more, as well as meet several other psychological measures of well-being.[15]

Effects of Income and Income Change on Happiness

Richard Easterlin pioneered the economics of "happiness" in the mid-1970s.[16] In a cross-country study using thirty surveys from nineteen countries, including developing countries, he found that in all cultures the way that most people spend their time is similar: working and trying to provide for their families. Thus the concerns that they express when asked about happiness are similar. His findings—that wealthy people tend to be happier than poorer ones within countries, but that there is no such relationship among countries or over time—have since been supported by a number of subsequent studies.[17]

To some extent, these findings are a puzzle. With economic growth and related improvements in living standards, such as reduced infant mortality and increased life expectancy, people are better off by any number of definitions. Yet these objective improvements do not seem to be captured in people's response to the happiness questions. Easterlin explained this apparent anomaly by suggesting that absolute income levels matter up to a certain point—particularly when basic needs are unmet—but after that, relative income differences matter more. (An additional explanation, discussed later, is that people's norms and expectations also adapt upward with eco-

15. See, for example, Diener and Biswas-Diener (2000).

16. Easterlin (1974) also finds that health is a demographic variable with clear effects on happiness in all societies, a finding that later studies corroborate. See also Easterlin (1995, 2000).

17. Easterlin (1974). See also Blanchflower and Oswald (1999), Diener (1984); Frey and Stutzer (2000). Deaton and Paxson (1994) highlight the role of negative shocks—such as poor health and bad luck—in determining lifetime mobility patterns. Such shocks, no doubt, also affect subjective assessments of well-being.

Figure 2-1. *Happiness and Income per Capita, Selected Countries, 1990s*[a]

Percent above neutral on life satisfaction

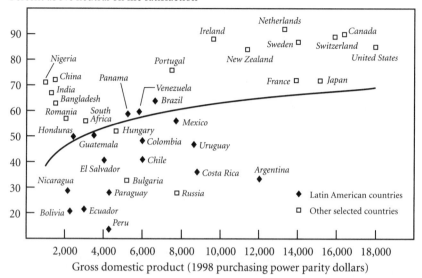

Gross domestic product (1998 purchasing power parity dollars)

Source: Authors' calculations based on Latinobarometro and Veenhoven world happiness data.
a. $R^2 = 0.14$.

nomic progress.) Later empirical studies support this proposition, showing a much stronger relation between income and happiness at the lower end of the income scale (figures 2-1 and 2-2).[18] Decades earlier, meanwhile, Pigou reasoned that because the rich derive much of their satisfaction from their relative, rather than absolute, income, satisfaction would not be reduced if the incomes of all the rich were diminished at the same time, justifying redistributive taxation.[19]

Ed Diener and his colleagues explored whether absolute or relative differences matter more to subjective well-being from the perspective of psychologists. They based their analysis on two samples: a cross-section of

18. Some scholars also find an additional effect at the very top of the scale, which might be explained by greed or changing preferences resulting from high levels of wealth. See Argyle (1999). Veenhoven (1991) meanwhile, finds that the correlation between income and happiness is much greater in poor countries. Recent work by Namazie and Sanfey (1998) in the transition economy of Kyrgyzstan confirms this. Frey and Stutzer (1999) find that at low and medium levels of income (for Switzerland), higher income has no effect on happiness, while above a specific income level, it does have some effect.

19. Pigou (1920, p. 53).

Figure 2-2. *Income Groups and Happiness in the United States, 1991–93*[a]

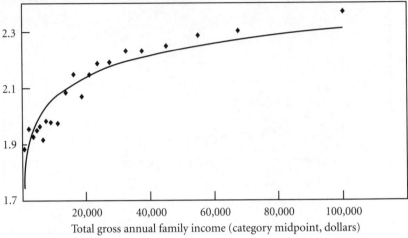

Mean happiness

Total gross annual family income (category midpoint, dollars)

Source: Authors' calculations from ICPSR.
a. $R^2 = 0.84$.

18,000 college students in thirty-nine countries (primarily developed economies), and a ten-year (1971–81) longitudinal study of 4,942 adults in the United States. They found a curvilinear relationship between income and happiness, in which there is a stronger relationship at the lower end of the income scale, and a flatter one at higher incomes that are well above subsistence levels. Across countries, they found a moderate relationship between affluence and life satisfaction.[20] Their findings highlight the importance of relative differences but do not discount the importance of absolute levels of income for happiness, even after people have incomes above the subsistence level.

They also examined income change. Across countries, they found that rapid economic growth is accompanied by less, not more, happiness.[21] When they looked at the effects of income changes at the individual level, they found that these do not yield additional effects on happiness beyond

20. Diener and others (1993) also make the point that the perceived discrepancies may not be driving the unhappiness, but rather that unhappy people are more likely to perceive differences.
21. See also Diener and Biswas-Diener (1999); and Diener and Suh (1999).

that of income levels. In other words, there are already some effects of income levels, which diminish as income goes up. There could also be additional effects of *changes* in income. To explain this, they posited that aspirations or "reference" norms may rise as fast as income, and thus objective increases in income make little difference. Although they did not have data on perceptions, they suggested that unhappiness might be driven more by perceived discrepancies in income change (that is, people perceiving that they make less than someone else, even though they might be making the same or more) than by actual income changes. (They also note that the direction of causality is not clear, as unhappy people may be more likely to perceive unfavorable discrepancies). This analysis of the effects of real and perceived income changes is quite relevant to our own empirical analysis, which finds that in developing economies, large, positive real income changes are accompanied by lower levels of perceived well-being for a significant percentage of the respondents in our surveys (see discussion in chapter 5).

The Role of Reference Norms

The importance of relative income differences to perceived well-being depends in part on social norms, which vary among societies. Under some norms, some societies, such as the United States, are more willing to tolerate higher levels of inequality in exchange for benefits (real or perceived) such as greater freedom or opportunity.[22] The basic tenet of the POUM hypothesis is that individuals' perceived prospects for future upward mobility, which are in part an outgrowth of cultural norms, are important determinants of their attitudes toward redistribution and other policies to reduce inequality.

Easterlin noted that while the aspirations of higher-income people probably exceed those of lower-income people, this dispersion in reference norms is smaller than is the dispersion in the actual incomes of the rich or poor. Thus those at the bottom tend to feel less well off. And as economic conditions improve over time, so do the reference norms, so that the positive correlation between higher income and well-being that shows up within

22. For a thoughtful review of different societies' tolerance for inequality, see Esping-Andersen (1990). For an excellent overview of trends in mobility and opportunity in the United States, see McMurrer and Sawhill (1998).

countries appears only weakly, if at all, in comparisons among societies in time or space.[23]

Easterlin's findings on the changing nature of norms and aspirations are supported by the work of Robert Merton, who introduced the concept of reference groups in his 1957 analysis of Stouffer's *American Soldier*. The latter is a comprehensive sociological study of the behavior of American soldiers both during and after combat, conducted in the 1940s.[24] Using Stouffer's data, Merton found that people's aspirations—and therefore their satisfaction or happiness—are very much determined by the reference group to which they compare themselves. A sample of soldiers was asked the question: "Do you think a soldier with ability has good chances for promotion?" The finding, in very general terms, was that the less the opportunity afforded by a branch for promotion, the more favorable the response about opportunities for promotion. This held for each level of longevity, rank, and education. Infantrymen, for example, whose cohorts were rarely promoted, reported higher scores of satisfaction with promotion opportunities than did their more upwardly mobile counterparts in the Air Force. Because promotion and upward mobility were the norm for Air Force men—indeed the Air Force had a noticeably high rate of promotion—and they assessed their own progress according to that of their peers, a higher percentage were dissatisfied with their own progress—even when they were upwardly mobile—than were infantrymen.[25] Our own findings are similar to Merton's: a significant percentage of our most upwardly mobile respondents report dissatisfaction with their progress.

Stouffer's data, based exclusively on men in different ranks in the military, allow us to distinguish clearly the particular reference group each respondent was comparing himself to: infantryman to infantrymen and Air Force man to Air Force men. The issue obviously becomes more complicated when the reference or comparison group is not clearly identifiable, as

23. In contrast very little is known about the effects of aggregate *declines* in income on reference norms. For an excellent account of how norms can shift downward, see Milanovic and Jovanovic (1999).

24. The authors are grateful to George Akerlof for helping them develop this line of analysis. See the chapter on "The American Soldier" in Merton (1957), particularly "Case Study 1," p. 236.

25. Similarly, Ravallion and Loshkin (1999a) find that relative differences matter a great deal: controlling for income and other factors, they find that living in wealthier neighborhoods lowers perceived social welfare.

is more likely in the less structured world outside the military. Our own samples, for example, are representative of large developing societies, and thus the reference groups of the upwardly mobile are much less clear.

At about the same time that Merton wrote his book, James Duesenberry was exploring the relationship between income aspirations and social status. His specific interest was in ascertaining how this relationship influences savings behavior, but the empirical work on which he based his analysis was remarkably similar to Merton's work. He relied on sociological research based in public opinion polls in the United States in the 1940s. A representative sample of 1,165 persons were asked to give their weekly income and answer the question: "About how much more money than that (the stated weekly income) do you think your family would need to have the things that might make your family happier or more comfortable than it is now?" The *percentage* increase people said they would need fell steadily as income increased until the highest group was reached: the lowest-income group (less than $20 weekly) wanted a 162 percent increase, the fourth highest group ($60–99 weekly) wanted a 52 percent increase, and the highest group (more than $100 weekly) wanted a 100 percent increase.[26] Duesenberry used this and data from other studies to test his theory that people who associated with others who had more income tended to be less satisfied with their income than were people who associated with others who were at the same income level.

In an extensive review of the subjective well-being studies conducted by psychologists—primarily but not exclusively in developed economies—Ed Diener and Robert Biswas-Diener found that people who prize material goals more than other values tend to be substantially less happy. They also find that winning lotteries tends to cause disruption rather than increased happiness. A plausible explanation is that such large income boosts may result in people purchasing nicer homes and other luxury goods that place them in a new reference group and among new neighbors, where they do not fit in.[27]

Other studies of happiness support the proposition that relative income differences and reference groups have stronger effects than absolute ones. Michalos's "goal achievement model" posits that happiness derives from the gap between aspirations and achievements and that this gap derives from

26. Duesenberry (1949, pp. 47–50).
27. Diener and Biswas-Diener (1999). On the lotteries point, see Argyle (1999).

comparisons both with "average folks" and one's own past life.[28] Clark and Oswald calculate "comparison incomes" for British workers: the average incomes of those with the same jobs, education, and so on. They found that while incomes had small effects on satisfaction, comparison income had a correlation of −.26 to −.31: the lower their comparison income, the more satisfied employees were. They also find that satisfaction with pay was lower if spouses or other household members earned more.[29]

The importance placed on relative income and reference groups can lead to an ever-rising bar of perceived needs, meanwhile. In a classic work, *The Theory of the Leisure Class*, Thorstein Veblen posits that in affluent societies, spending—and in particular conspicuous consumption—becomes the vehicle through which people establish social position. Several decades later, Juliet Schor cites repeated surveys showing that more than half of the population of the United States, the richest population in the world, say they cannot afford everything they really need.[30]

A relative definition of economic well-being has also been used to explain social unrest and political violence in many countries. Ted Gurr, in an oft-cited study based on evidence from experimental psychologists, case studies of rebellions, and a large database on conflict-related deaths from 114 countries, cites relative deprivation as "the basic, instigating condition for participants in collective violence. . . . Societal conditions that increase the average level or intensity of expectations without increasing capabilities increase the intensity of discontent. Among the general conditions that have such effects are the value gains of other groups and the promise of new opportunities."[31] And, as noted above, Hirschman's tunnel effect hypothesis argues that timing matters: an initial increase in income inequality can raise hope and expectation, but persistent inequality can lead to increased frustration and feelings of relative deprivation.

28. Michalos (1980), as discussed in Argyle (1999). Other authors find that the theory works only for realistic aspirations, or those under one's own control. Comparison with the past seems important as a "reality check" of sorts. See Argyle (1999).

29. Clark and Oswald (1996); see also Oswald (1997).

30. Veblen (1967); Schor (1998).

31. Gurr (1970) relies on his own well-known database on conflict-related violence, as well as earlier data for pre-1948 conflicts from Richardson (1960). Gurr has significantly expanded that data set, which is available on the University of Maryland website (www.bsos.umd.edu/cidcm/mar).

Other Factors Affecting Happiness

David Blanchflower and Andrew Oswald compare happiness in the United States and in Britain, using data from the 1970s through the 1990s from the U.S. General Social Survey and from the Eurobarometer survey. They also examine effects of macroeconomic variables on happiness.[32] They find that unemployment and poor health have negative effects on happiness, whereas marriage has a strong positive effect. Indeed, the single greatest depressant on happiness is the variable "separated," closely followed by "widowed," and then by "unemployed." Education, independent of income, has a positive effect on happiness. And while income also has positive effects, these are not as large as those of the nonincome variables. Di Tella, MacCulloch, and Oswald find that inflation has very strong negative effects on happiness and that people are willing to undergo very costly recessions (and thereby implicitly forgo considerable income) to get rid of inflation.

Bruno Frey and Alois Stutzer explore the relationship between income and happiness among 6,000 residents in Switzerland's cantons. Like Blanchflower and Oswald, they find that unemployment and poor health have clear negative effects on happiness. Self-employed people are happier than employees. Inflation has a negative effect on happiness. Frey and Stutzer also explore the effects of direct democracy on happiness. All residents in Swiss cantons receive public goods, but only Swiss nationals can participate politically. Controlling for differences in quality of public goods among the cantons, they find that happiness levels are higher among the Swiss nationals who take part in direct democracy than in the foreign residents who only benefit from the public goods it provides. (Of course, other factors that are more difficult to measure may be affecting the happiness of foreigners in Switzerland, such as subtle discrimination and the absence of family living nearby).[33]

Our own work on Latin America corroborates the findings of the negative effects of unemployment and inflation on happiness (detailed results

32. See Blanchflower and Oswald (1999); Di Tella, MacCulloch, and Oswald (1997).

33. We are grateful to George Akerlof for making this point. Frey and Stutzer (1999) also find that married people are happier than single people, that couples without children are happier than those with them, and that women are happier than men. For the same issues in the transition economies, see Namazie and Sanfey (1998).

are in chapter 4 and table 4-3).[34] We obtain slightly different findings for self-employment, however. Using data from the Latinobarometro, we found that controlling for other variables, being self-employed had no significant effects on happiness for those in the wealthiest socioeconomic category, but a significant and *negative* effect for those in the middle and poor categories. This is not surprising, as those who are self-employed in developed economies usually have chosen to be, whereas most of those who are poor and self-employed in developing countries are in the informal sector because they lack other alternatives.[35]

Charles Kenny explores the links between happiness and economic growth, using a sample of advanced industrial countries for which there are happiness surveys from the 1950s through the 1990s.[36] Like Easterlin, he notes the importance of relative, rather than absolute, income differences in people's self-assessments. He finds that, at least in wealthy countries, any existing link between growth and happiness runs from happiness to growth rather than the other way around. This linkage may result from a social interactions effect: trust and social capital seem to be greater in "happier" societies, and a number of studies have found positive associations between these two variables and growth.

Kenny also notes that the nature of utility matters: utility measures desire, not satisfaction, and a nonrational actor, like King Midas, may be moving up to higher indifference curves in pursuit of desires that do not satisfy him. The measurement of happiness or subjective well-being entails all sorts of factors, including social norms, social interactions, neighborhood effects, and the economics of identity.[37] The criteria that a young male member of a gang uses to assess his well-being are probably quite different from those used by a similarly aged graduate of Yale, even though both live in the same country where the sort of norm-sharing that Easterlin referred to is in operation.

---

34. Moulton (1990) identifies a potential downward bias in standard errors as a problem when estimating the effects of aggregate variables on small units. Assuming errors on the order of those Moulton finds in his analysis, most of our results would still hold.

35. For more detail, see Graham and Pettinato (2001).

36. Kenny's study covers primarily European countries, plus the United States and Japan, and is based on the Veenhoven happiness data set. For details, see Kenny (1999).

37. For work on social interactions and neighborhood effects, see, for example, Durlauf (forthcoming [b]). For the role of identity in influencing economic behavior, see Akerlof and Kranton (2000).

Along these lines, William Foote Whyte examines the behavior of youths and their groups in an Italian slum in Boston: clubs for college-bound boys; and gangs for the boys who remain on the street-corner. He shows how norms can derive from social interactions established in early boyhood. Some of the boys who were excluded from the gangs were freer and more motivated to leave the slum and pursue higher education and successful careers than were gang members. Gangs, more than clubs, are tight networks of reciprocal obligations, which can become social traps. Yet reported satisfaction in the gangs is about the same as it is among the college boys.[38]

A few economists have attempted to develop measures of individual welfare that capture its subjective elements. Bernard Van Praag's measure—now known as the Leyden approach—assesses the interaction between individual preferences and the effects of social norms and the incomes of others. His measure also attempts to capture the effects of changes over time, showing that anticipated income gains have greater effects on individuals' subjective well-being than do the actual gains themselves; indeed in retrospect the individual may even be disappointed at the size or effects of the gains. These evaluations are also affected by changes in norms, or what Van Praag and colleagues term the social standard income. Thus welfare or utility depends not only on present income but also on future income, and experienced and anticipated incomes contribute to the formation of the present norm on incomes.[39]

Empirical research, based on cross-country surveys and using these measures, finds that individual welfare functions differ among individuals, depending on their stage in the life cycle. Overall, current income has the greatest weight, followed by past income, and then anticipated future income. The weights given each category vary by age, however, with the young and the old placing the greatest weight on past income, whereas the middle-age bracket derives its norm mostly from current and anticipated income.[40] A similar subjectivity affects individuals' evaluations of age and education. People's definition of "young," for example, tends to change as

38. Foote Whyte (1993).
39. Van Praag developed the Leyden approach in 1971. For detail, see Van Praag and Frijters (1999).
40. Van Praag and Frijters (1999). Meanwhile, Lowenstein, Prelec, and Weber (1999) find that people grow unhappier as they anticipate retiring, but that happiness levels increase shortly after retirement.

they age. Other research on assessments of quality of life, meanwhile, finds that as people age and their reference norms are others in their age cohort, their reference norms for health status bias downward. Wim Groot uses a representative sample of the British population, based on the 1995 Household Panel Survey, to derive quality-adjusted life-year (QALY) weights from the effects of actual health status of individuals on their subjective health. He finds that ill people tend to adapt their quality-of-life assessments upward, as their reference norms become either others with the same illness or an earlier stage of their illness that was more critical.[41]

Another measurement issue in assessing subjective well-being, which is as much in the domain of psychologists as of social scientists, is the direction of causality: are people happy because of their economic conditions, or do happy people assess their economic conditions more favorably?[42] This is a question that will only be answered with future research, and then probably by psychologists rather than economists. There is clear evidence that respondents' assessments are often affected by the momentary mood of individuals at the time of interview, which can be affected by events such as the fate of the national football team or a recent election. These same factors can affect recall, and people often recall past events in a manner that supports their current assessments.[43]

Finally, there is also the question of how "happiness" affects economic behavior and therefore future income. Diener and Biswas-Diener report findings from a panel survey from Australia: high subjective well-being scores at an earlier time period precede increasing income, with one standard deviation increase in subjective well-being producing 2 to 3 percentage point increases in income, and two standard deviations resulting in 8 to 12 percentage points greater income increases in the next time period. They also report results from studies in the United States that found positive

41. Such a period could be the stage before a kidney transplant, for example, rather than the stage before the illness occurred; see Groot (2000). Other work also suggests that poor people are much less likely than wealthy ones to report health problems.

42. In a theoretical analysis, Koszegi (2000) shows that people who assess their capabilities optimistically are also likely to process information in a biased manner, that is, in a way that supports their optimistic assessments; in the most extreme cases, some stop seeking out information altogether.

43. For detail on measurement issues, see Diener (1984).

effects of cheerfulness on later incomes; these results were moderated by respondents' parents' income, however; the effects were greater for individuals from economically advantaged backgrounds.[44]

The effects of happiness or subjective well-being on future economic—and possibly also political—behavior is an area where much more theoretical and empirical work is needed. Such work will ultimately determine the importance of the study of subjective well-being to future social science research and policy.[45]

Mobility and Voting

One way of gauging how people assess their current well-being and their future prospects for advancement is how they behave politically, in particular, how they vote on issues pertaining to redistribution. Theorists and policymakers closely debate the role of redistribution in mitigating relative income differences and building political support for market policies.

A commonly held view is that implementing redistributive policies entails efficiency tradeoffs and that reducing inequality always has efficiency costs.[46] A less common view highlights strategies that avoid both the efficiency costs and the political risks associated with redistributive programs and instead focus on removing market distortions that cause or exacerbate inequality and entail their own efficiency costs. An example of such a distortion is rationed credit in the financial sector, which favors large and politically powerful borrowers, while limiting the capacity of the poor to save and invest.[47]

An underlying assumption in both scenarios in that there are political risks as well as efficiency costs associated with redistribution. Pathbreaking work by Alberto Alesina and Roberto Perotti, for example, demonstrates formally how high inequality can lead to political instability, populist economic policies, and ultimately lower growth, as the median voter (whose income level is below the mean) opts for high levels of redistribution, which

44. Diener and Biswas-Diener (1999).
45. Thaler (2000), discussing the future of economics, cited emotion as one of three areas that the profession had to incorporate more integrally into its analysis.
46. See, among others, Okun (1975).
47. See Birdsall, Graham, and Sabot (1998).

in turn undermines investor confidence.[48] In this and other work on inequality and voting, based on current income levels and median voter theory, higher levels of inequality almost always lead to more political support for redistribution.

In contrast, work that focuses on income mobility rather than on static and aggregate measures of the distribution of income offers a different interpretation of the political economy of redistribution. Benabou and Ok explicitly argue in their POUM hypothesis that individuals' perceived prospects of upward mobility explain limited support for redistribution, even when the median voter is well below the average in terms of income.[49] Their theoretical analysis, supported with empirical evidence from the United States, depicts tomorrow's income as a concave function of today's. The coalition in favor of laissez-faire is larger the more concave the transition function, the longer the duration of the proposed tax scheme, and the more far-sighted the voters. Either set of assumptions is plausible given a particular context, but the focus on perceptions of future mobility is more relevant to our own analysis and findings.[50]

In more recent work, Alesina and colleagues Rafael Di Tella and Robert MacCulloch, using survey data from the Eurobarometer and U.S. General Social Survey, find that inequality has very different effects on happiness in the United States than in Europe.[51] In general, inequality has no effects on

48. Alesina and Perotti (1994). Pettinato (2000) compiles evidence from a broader collection of data and research that blurs the relationship between inequality and growth more than it is in a pure cross-country analysis. More attention to data comparability and quality, as well as to analytical techniques used, may show a more complex picture.

49. See Benabou and Ok (1998). For a more philosophical discussion of why U.S. citizens support high levels of inequality and do not vote for more taxation, a discussion that supports the basic premises of Benabou and Ok, see Okun (1975). (Rather ironically, POUM is also the acronym for the Catalonian Marxist Party, the *Partido Obrero Unificado Marxista*, which the author George Orwell joined during the Spanish Civil War. The authors would like to thank Alan Angell for calling this point to their attention.)

50. An interesting empirical contrast is highlighted by Martin Ravallion's recent research in Russia, which finds a strong demand for redistribution stemming from most Russians' (accurate) expectations of declining living standards and mobility in the future. See Ravallion and Loshkin (1999b).

51. In the United States they look at intrastate inequality; in Europe, at intracountry inequality. For the United States they use the Gini coefficients of gross family income for each state from the Census Bureau; for Europe they use Gini coefficients from the 1996 Deininger and Squire data set, accepting that there are problems related to different methods used in different countries to calculate the Ginis. All of them rely on household survey data and have nationally representative samples. See Alesina, Di Tella, and MacCulloch (2000).

happiness in the United States, according to their findings, yet when they split their sample by socioeconomic status and political leanings, they find that the only group in the United States whose happiness is negatively affected by inequality are the rich who lean to the left! In contrast in Europe, inequality has stronger negative effects on the happiness of both the poor and those on the left compared with those from other socioeconomic groups and political orientations. Alesina and his colleagues suggest that the explanation lies in the higher rates of social mobility (both real and perceived) in the United States.

Five years before Benabou and Ok's work appeared, Thomas Piketty offered another political economy model based on mobility rather than current income. Piketty argued that individual mobility experiences are key to political attitudes and that differences in perceptions about social mobility can generate persistent differences in income distribution patterns across countries.[52]

Piketty's argument had been foreshadowed a century earlier by Alexis de Tocqueville, who attributed different attitudes toward redistribution in the United States and Europe to their respective mobility rates. Piketty cited the importance of social origins and mobility experiences: he found that voters with the exact same incomes but different social origins vote differently on redistribution. These differences are particularly strong at the extreme tails of the distribution, that is, stable low-income and high-income voters are very likely to maintain their political identities (such as conservative or liberal, left or right), while upwardly and downwardly mobile groups in the middle are more likely to shift identities. Research by Clifford and Heath, based on data from the United Kingdom, applies a hypothesis of asymmetric mobility: those who are upwardly mobile usually adopt the political behavior (usually conservative) of the class they arrive in, while the downwardly mobile continue to associate with the class that they came from.[53]

Piketty shows how attitudes generated by past mobility experiences have persistent effects on future economic behavior and can account for widening inequality. Even without redistribution, inequality for a given homogeneous cohort can grow with age. The only inequality among young people

52. Piketty (1995).
53. Clifford and Heath (1993).

who start out with the same beliefs and put forward the same degree of effort comes from economic shocks. But as time passes, people who have experienced negative shocks may become (rationally) discouraged and supply less effort, while more successful people keep putting out more effort. Eventually, inequality persists because of the dynamics of endogenous beliefs (those that grow out of each individual's experience).[54]

In this book we contend that both past mobility and prospects of upward mobility are factors in the political economy of market reform. Admittedly, noneconomic factors influence voters, and these effects may be less straightforward than the theory suggests. Still, attitudes about mobility may be significant variables explaining why voters in many countries have repeatedly voted for the continuation of laissez-faire or neoliberal economic policies despite the persistence and even increase of inequality. Indeed, our results, discussed in chapter 4, show that POUM levels (self-assessments of individual prospects of upward mobility) are higher in the more unequal countries early on in their reform programs. We also find that tolerance for inequality declines as the reform process consolidates, supporting Hirschman's hypothesis that the persistence of inequality is what causes frustration, not initial increases in inequality related to economic progress or change.

Mobility and Social Interactions

An additional focus of our analysis is the influence of social interactions on mobility and opportunity and, less directly, on public attitudes about redistribution. Social interactions can help determine mobility rates. Much has been written recently about the positive role of social capital on growth. Our view is that the effects are far less straightforward than is typically assumed. The definition of social capital is critical, and this definition hinges on the type of interaction at play. Much of the social capital literature assumes that social interactions are positive, whereas other research, such as that of Steven Durlauf and Karla Hoff, shows that some kinds of social interactions can result in poverty traps.[55]

54. Piketty (1995).
55. Durlauf (forthcoming [b]); Hoff (1996). Young (1999), meanwhile, finds that in many cases both the structure and strength of interactions, such as bilateral trading relationships,

Rather than focusing broadly on the relationship between social interactions and economic growth, we focus on mobility, as represented, for example, by income change. Our work suggests that upward mobility is not linked to participation in civic associations, broadly defined.[56] There are many possible reasons for this, including the opportunity costs of time spent associating; the kinds of links that these associations provide—or fail to provide—beyond the neighborhood; and the nature of the associations themselves. Many civic associations in developing countries arise out of shared necessity: soup kitchens, mothers' clubs, group credit schemes. Their purpose is to make up for the absence of adequate economic opportunities or safety nets.[57] Leaving the group means individuals lose the security benefits of membership to seek better opportunities outside. Those that do move on self-select according to their education levels, their degree of risk aversion, and available information and opportunities.

In contrast to these kinds of organizations are those that Putnam focused on in his original work on the topic: the voluntary associational arrangements that foster trust, transmit information, and ultimately contribute to economic growth.[58] These are distinct from the survival organizations of the poor in two ways. First, members choose to associate voluntarily rather than as a last resort. Second, these groups have different ties with the rest of society than do the survival organizations. Granovetter distinguishes between strong ties, or kinship and friendships, which provide horizontal linkages within organizations or local groups, and weak ties, or networks, which provide bridges to other groups and associations beyond the locale.[59] His empirical work, based on interviews with U.S. blue- and white-collar workers, shows that weak ties are consistently the basis for upward mobility.

---

are endogenous to the context and can generate stochastically stable states that take a long time to undo. One implication of Young's work is that inequality generated by unequal bargaining positions and outcomes can persist between the networks of the rich and those of the poor.

56. See Putnam (1993). See also Knack and Keefer (1997).

57. For the central role played by such organizations in providing safety nets worldwide, see Graham (1994).

58. Putnam (1993). For a critical review of Putnam's later work, see Durlauf (forthcoming [a]).

59. See Granovetter (1973). We would like to thank Judith Tendler for raising this point in this context.

When we make this distinction between kinds of organizations in our own analysis, we find a link between upward mobility and participation in associations for noneconomic reasons. Our upwardly mobile respondents are less likely to be involved in group insurance or other joint survival schemes and are more likely to associate to seek weak ties: acquaintances and new contacts outside their immediate reference group.

Other authors have made related arguments. David Krackhardt, building on Granovetter's work, notes that weak ties provide access to information and resources beyond those available in their own social settings, while strong ties are better suited to providing assistance and adaptation to economic change and uncertainty.[60] The survival organizations of the poor are characterized by strong ties, yet weak ties are more likely to encourage upward mobility. Paul Collier defines social capital as social if it is an interaction that generates an externality and as capital if its economic effects are persistent.[61] Most organizations of the poor meet the former but not the latter criterion.

In empirical work in Central America, Amber Seligson finds that of the many kinds of civil society organizations that the poor belong to, only one, community development organizations, forges weak ties. They provide channels for making demands: to the local mayor, to the legislature, or to a relevant central government agency. Other organizations, such as church or school-related associations, are inward-looking and rarely need to move beyond their network to solve problems.[62]

In a longitudinal study of political behavior across poor neighborhoods in Peru, Henry Dietz finds that as economic pressures build, the poor turn their organizational activities from social mobilization and political demand making to inward-looking, neighborhood coping solutions. Their behavior becomes increasingly risk averse as the need to preserve economic security or income generation capacity increases.[63] Again, associational life is providing welfare externalities, but it is not encouraging upward mobility or economic growth. It may even be deterring it.

60. Krackhardt (1992).
61. Collier (1998).
62. Seligson (1999).
63. Dietz (1998).

Conclusion

Our attempt to explore the effects of income mobility—and perceptions of past and future mobility—on economic and political behavior in new market economies draws on several literatures from several disciplines. We have placed a particular emphasis on the role of the timing and persistence of relative income differences as developed by Hirschman in the tunnel hypothesis and on public expectations about future mobility as developed by Benabou and others in exploring the POUM hypothesis. Although all of these literatures have been invaluable in helping us conceptualize the core issues, empirical data, particularly for the developing economies, are in short supply. We hope that our analysis of such data, generated largely through survey research in Latin America, can contribute to several of these bodies of literature.

Given our emphasis in this book on public attitudes about relative income differences and about future opportunities for upward mobility, most of our research efforts are focused on mobility trends and public perceptions about those trends, as well as expectations for the future. Yet we believe that the role of social interactions and other kinds of peer effects on mobility as well as individual attitudes about mobility warrant further discussion and empirical exploration. Our methods for addressing these questions in our surveys, as well as our empirical results, are discussed in chapter 5.

Before discussing the effects of mobility on economic and political behavior and the effects of social interactions on that complex relationship, we provide a conceptual framework for thinking about mobility and then summarize what we know about mobility trends in the emerging market economies in chapter 3.

3

Concepts and Trends in Income Mobility

Few topics are as widely studied and debated as poverty and inequality. An enormous amount of territory has been covered in the effort to better understand these complex issues and the interactions between them.[1] Nonetheless, much more remains to be done, particularly on the interactions between poverty and inequality. The move toward global economic integration, meanwhile, has introduced additional variables—such as technology-led growth—that have significant effects on trends in poverty and inequality in addition to those of macroeconomic and public expenditure policies. Debate is widespread about the effects of these trends and about the ability of domestic policies to harness them in a manner that includes the poor in economic growth.

Traditional measures of poverty and inequality, such as the poverty head-count ratio and the Gini coefficient, do not capture much about what is happening over time or within the income distribution of any one society.[2]

---

1. This chapter draws heavily from Birdsall and Graham (2000), Graham (2000), and Birdsall, Graham, and Pettinato (2000).

2. The Gini coefficient measures the extent of a country's inequality based on the gap between its Lorenz curve and the 45 degree line representing a perfectly equal distribution. It does not capture short-term movements or those between adjacent income deciles very accurately. The Wolfson polarization index measures the degree to which income is concentrated

Table 3-1. *Markov Transition Matrices Examples*

Society A. No Income Mobility

Percent

Quintile in T_0	Quintile in T_1					
	1	2	3	4	5	Total
1	100	0	0	0	0	100
2	0	100	0	0	0	100
3	0	0	100	0	0	100
4	0	0	0	100	0	100
5	0	0	0	0	100	100
Total	100	100	100	100	100	100

Society B. Perfect Income Mobility

Percent

Quintile in T_0	Quintile in T_1					
	1	2	3	4	5	Total
1	20	20	20	20	20	100
2	20	20	20	20	20	100
3	20	20	20	20	20	100
4	20	20	20	20	20	100
5	20	20	20	20	20	100
Total	100	100	100	100	100	100

In other words, these measures do not show who is moving in and out of poverty and why, nor do they show differences in access to opportunity among societies with similar income distributions. Two societies with exactly the same Gini, for example, could be extremely different in terms of the mobility and opportunity individual members of society have during their lifetimes and also the amount of mobility and opportunity children have compared with their parents.

At one extreme, imagine a static society with no movement up and down the income ladder in a defined interval. In this society people who begin at the top of the distribution remain there over time, and those who begin at the bottom stay there. Even worse, that static distribution could be transmitted across generations, with the children of the poor also remaining poor. This society is depicted as society A in the transition matrix in table 3-1, where the same people who begin in a certain quintile in time zero are also there in time one. This is a society with no income mobility.

At the other extreme, imagine a society with complete mobility, where the probability of staying in the same quintile in which one starts is identical to that of moving to any other quintile; in this example, some of those who begin at the top may end up at the bottom, and some who begin at the bottom may finish at the top. This is society B in table 3-1. In theory, this is

---

at the top and bottom. Income skewness, as defined by Lindert (1996), is the difference in size between the gap between the rich and the middle and that between the middle and the poor.

the sort of distribution of opportunity (although not of outcomes) envisioned by philosopher John Rawls. In his maximin criterion, those entrusted with designing the structure of society and the distribution of opportunities must do so with a veil of ignorance about their own inherited advantages, so that they have no incentive to perpetuate a social structure that favors the privileged.[3] (The *outcome* envisioned by Rawls might have had less mobility than this society, if with complete mobility some people are moving from low to lower quintiles.)[4]

In reality, a country with complete mobility is difficult to imagine. Nor is it clear that most people would accept a situation where they could not pass things on to their children, be they genetic endowments, educational opportunities, or used cars. In the real world, a number of parental characteristics do determine their children's fates. Although some of these, such as genetic endowments, are beyond human control and are integral to innovation and diversity, others, such as income, education, and employment opportunities, are the result of economic and social phenomena over which public policy does have some influence.

There is a great deal of debate—and diversity among societies—about how aggressive public policy should be in leveling the playing field. Some societies value the public school system as a guarantee of equal opportunity, while others emphasize individual effort and parental choices as important individual rights.The extremes, for example, are caste systems or feudal societies that deny access to education to certain sectors of society versus the egalitarian Scandinavian countries, where access to high levels of high-quality education is almost universal. Some societies tax inheritances almost to nonexistence, while in others, such intergenerational transfers are considered as sacred as the transfer of family names or lineage.[5]

There is no correct formula for resolving such debates, nor is there a model society. It is possible, however, to identify the factors that block opportunity and mobility for the poor and result in the intergenerational transmission of poverty, something that is not desirable in any society. Moreover, international economic integration and the adoption of market reforms in several developing countries provide numerous opportunities to

3. Rawls (1971).
4. We thank an anonymous reviewer for clarifying this point.
5. See Stiglitz (2000).

enhance the mobility of low-income groups, but these trends also introduce new vulnerabilities, such as rapidly changing returns to different skill levels, that static measures may not fully capture. Although the debate on globalization and market reforms has centered on the effects of these trends on poverty and inequality, as captured by static measures, much less, if any, attention has been paid to their effects on mobility and opportunity.

The Importance of Mobility: Measuring Inequality over Time

We think a focus on mobility is warranted for several reasons. First, the concept of mobility is better suited to evaluating the effects of policy changes, such as market reforms, on poverty and inequality than are traditional static measures. For example, several years or even decades may pass before aggregate distributions, as measured by the Gini, register any change. Yet individuals can have substantial movements up and down the income ladder—often as a result of policy changes—in the course of a year or two. Second, patterns in mobility rates over time may well provide information about longer-term distributive trends. Poverty headcount ratios and other traditional poverty measures, meanwhile, tell little about how far out of poverty individuals are able to move, why they are able to move up, and how permanent those movements are.

Finally, the increasing importance of globalization and technology-driven growth has led to significant changes in the determinants of mobility, such as widening gaps between the rewards to skilled and unskilled labor as well as to higher education versus primary and secondary education. Understanding these changes will be critical to addressing poverty and inequality in the future. One reason for the lack of attention to this issue to date is the paucity of data on mobility trends, which require following the same individual over extended periods of time. Thus new and better data will also be necessary to advance this agenda.

We are concerned with two distinct aspects of mobility, neither of which is easily captured in conventional measures of income inequality. The first is lifetime income and mobility. The incomes of lawyers in the United States for example, when measured at one point in time, are extremely unequal, as most recently graduated lawyers are heavily in debt while more experienced lawyers have high incomes relative to other occupations. The lifetime income profiles of lawyers, however, are much more equal. Annual measures of

Figure 3-1. *Earnings of Lawyers and Bricklayers Compared over Time*

Earnings

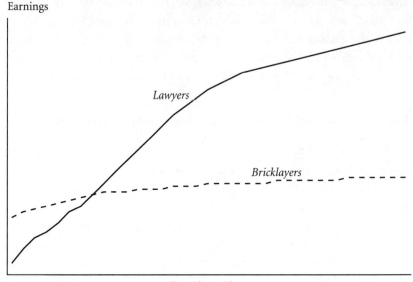

Experience/time

bricklayers' incomes, meanwhile, are likely to be far more equal, but their lifetime profiles will demonstrate a much smaller change in distribution, because their earnings opportunities do not increase as much with time as do those of lawyers (figure 3-1). Obviously, in economies undergoing major structural change, the situation is more complicated: many people will change occupations during their lifetime, some occupations will emerge and others disappear, and the lifetime income profiles of different occupations may change dramatically.

Typical measures of inequality say nothing, for example, about lawyers' or bricklayers' lifetime income or mobility. Measures of inequality are like snapshots; they reflect differences in income at a specific point in time—but not whether individuals are moving up or down the income ladder or expect to do so. These measures therefore say little about what is happening to people's opportunities and to their well-being over a prolonged period of policy change.

A second measure of inequality is intergenerational, for example, across members of different generations within a family. Societies differ in the extent of their intergenerational mobility, that is, the extent to which the position of parents (and grandparents and so on) in the income or other ranking of their generation determines the position of their children (and grandchildren and so on). At one time, land ownership or bloodline mattered most. With the global turn to the market, education appears to be the factor that matters most, and thus some combination of public and parental investment in children's education determines intergenerational mobility.[6]

Lifetime income mobility is likely to be influenced by business cycle volatility, and intergenerational mobility by structural changes in economies such as the opening of trade markets and divestiture of state-owned enterprises.[7] In the longer term, patterns of mobility are also influenced by broader secular trends in the global economy. During the industrialization of the nineteenth century, economic opportunities and rewards were largely determined by a capital-labor divide. With the turn to high technology growth, a similar divide exists between educated and uneducated workers, enhancing the opportunities and rewards of the former, and decreasing the returns to the labor of the latter.

We argue that individuals' assessments of their well-being are more likely to be influenced by their mobility—both intra- and intergenerational—than by aggregate and static measures of inequality, such as trends in the Gini coefficient in their particular country. We also contend that their assessments are influenced by the fate of other individuals, particularly those in their reference groups. Moreover, awareness of how others are faring has increased with the spread of technology and global information, and it is likely that increasing numbers of individuals in the developing world are aware of how they are faring relative to those within and beyond their reference groups.

Trends: What Is Known and Unknown about Mobility

Although measuring mobility is conceptually appealing, doing so accurately is difficult. Accurate measurements require data about specific individuals over prolonged periods of time—this is, panel data. Many advanced

---

6. There is a wide literature on this issue. For detail and references, see Sawhill (2000); Behrman, Birdsall, and Székely (2000b).

7. Behrman (2000).

industrial countries have at least one nationally representative panel survey, but these surveys, which are expensive to develop and maintain, are rare for developing countries. Some panel data are available for particular periods in individual developing countries, but it is impossible to reproduce panel data for past time periods for which they do not exist. We therefore must infer, where possible, broader patterns and trends from the sparse data available.[8] Based on these inferences, what we see with globalization is an increase in mobility and opportunity on the one hand and an increase in vulnerability on the other.

The few studies that examine mobility at the household level in developing countries are suggestive.[9] In Indonesia data on the variability of annual household spending suggest that many households in the middle of the income distribution have a high probability of having been poor or becoming poor. Assuming 20 percent of households are poor, an additional 30 percent are "vulnerable" to becoming poor over three years. Moreover, when the sample is divided between urban and rural households, the urban households—on average less poor—are nearly as vulnerable as the rural ones.[10] In China in the second half of the 1980s, the distinction between being poor and not being poor disappeared for almost half of all households. Although only 6.2 percent of the population was poor for the entire period, 54 percent was poor during at least one year. The corresponding figures for Zimbabwe (1993 to 1996) are 10.6 and 59.6 percent.[11]

Data following panels of households in Peru also reveal remarkable movement up and down the income ladder. Trends in relative income mobility are shown as a Markov transition matrix in table 3-2. The table is divided into income quintiles, with the rows being the quintile of origin in 1991 and the columns being the quintile of destination in 2000. The figures

8. For a comprehensive review of the literature and the kinds of data available on mobility, see Yaqub (2000).

9. The study of mobility has been much further developed by sociologists than by economists. For a review of the state of the art in economic mobility studies and how the existing concepts and measures apply to the emerging market countries, see Birdsall and Graham (2000).

10. Pritchett, Suryahadi, and Sumarto (2000).

11. Ethiopia more closely fits the commonly, though wrongly, perceived pattern. The 1994–95 figures there are 24.8 and 30.1 percent, respectively; see Baulch and Hoddinott (2000). Several other countries are covered in this study, but the length of the panels—less than one year—or the more limited nature of the data (rural Chile only) precluded their being discussed in detail here.

Table 3-2. *Relative Mobility in Peru, 1991–2000*[a]

Percent

Quintile 1991	Quintile 2000					
	1	2	3	4	5	Total
1	45	25	19	6	5	100
2	25	25	23	14	13	100
3	16	23	22	20	19	100
4	11	18	18	32	21	100
5	3	9	18	28	42	100
Total	100	100	100	100	100	100

Source: Authors' calculations from Cuánto, S. A. (1999).
a. Quintiles are calculated using equivalence expenditure.

are in percentages; thus 100 percent in the same row and column would imply complete immobility, and 20 percent would represent evenly distributed mobility.

The matrix shows substantial mobility for those in the Peru panel. Households in the third and fourth quintiles clearly experienced the most downward mobility, with 39 percent of those in the third and 47 percent of those in the fourth moving to lower quintiles between 1991 and 2000. Those that experienced the most—and most intense—upward mobility were in the first and second quintiles (the poorest), with 55 and 50 percent, respectively, moving up, and a significant percentage of these moving up two or even three quintiles. In addition to the effects of demographics, education, individual effort, and stochastic factors such as luck, these trends reflect the benefits to the poor from stabilizing hyperinflation, the targeting of public expenditures to the poorest groups, and changes in opportunity generated by high growth after inflation was stabilized.[12]

In terms of absolute mobility, the majority of households in the panel—58 percent—had income increases of 30 percent or more from 1991 through 2000.[13] Another 30 percent had only marginal income changes, and 12 percent had income drops of 30 percent or more. Looking at these

12. For detail on government policies at the time, see Graham and Kane (1998).
13. This is measured on the basis of household expenditure data in Lima 2000 prices, which is adjusted for household size using a one-parameter equivalence scale with elasticity of 0.5. For details on the implications in using this or other equivalence methods, see Figini (1998).

Box 3-1. *Changes in Log-Income vs. Income*
The following example illustrates the different effects of using log-income instead of income. Consider four individuals with different levels of income (y) who experience an identical percentage increase of income (50 percent) in two different moments in time:

Time	Poor y	Poor $log(y)$	Middle income y	Middle income $log(y)$	Rich y	Rich $log(y)$	Very rich y	Very rich $log(y)$
0	2	0.30	20	1.30	200	2.30	2000	3.30
1	3	0.48	30	1.48	300	2.48	3000	3.48

The same percentage change has a higher impact on the poor person's utility than on the very rich person's utility. The following formulation allows us to capture this difference: the percentage change in log-income.

Income-mobility measure for individual i from time 0 to 1 =

$$\frac{\log(y)1_i - \log(y)0_i}{\log(y)0_i}.$$

Although the simple percentage change in income produces a value of 50 percent across the board, the log-income measure produces gains of 58 percent for the poor person, 14 percent for the middle-class individual, 8 percent for the rich person, and 5 percent for the very rich person, reflecting the decreasing impact of the same percentage change in income on utility as the initial income level of the individual increases.

mobility trends logarithmically, we find that our mobility trends, which were on balance positive, had greater significance for those at the bottom end of the income ladder.[14] (For an explanation of log-income compared with income, see box 3-1.)

14. To do this, we used a measure developed by Gary Fields: $1/N \Sigma_i \ln x_i - \ln y_i$, where N is the total number of households and x and y are the final and initial expenditure levels. In Peru

Table 3-3. *Relative Mobility in the United States, 1979–1989*[a]

Percent

	Quintile 1989					
Quintile 1979	1	2	3	4	5	Total
1	61	24	9	5	1	100
2	23	33	28	14	3	100
3	8	25	30	26	11	100
4	5	13	23	33	26	100
5	3	5	11	23	59	100
Total	100	100	100	100	100	100

Source: Mishel, Bernstein, and Schmitt (1999).
a. Quintiles are calculated using family income.

Comparing the data from Peru with panel data from the United States for 1979 through 1989 demonstrates the greater movement in both upward and downward mobility in Peru. Tables 3-2 and 3-3 show positional mobility (that is, mobility across groups defined in relative terms) in the two countries. In Peru 42 percent of those in the richest quintile in 1991 were still there in 2000, while 59 percent of those in the wealthiest quintile in the United States in 1979 stayed there. In Peru only 45 percent of those who started in the bottom quintile were still there at the end of the period, while 61 percent of those who started at the bottom in the United States were still there at the end of the period. And of those who started in Peru's bottom quintile, 6 percent made it all the way to the fourth quintile, while 5 percent made it to the fifth quintile.[15] The same percentages for the United States are

---

between 1991 and 1994 log-expenditure increased by 0.339 units on average; see Fields and Ok (1999). The corresponding figure for the 1994–96 period shows a dramatic average decline of –0.334, while the 1996–2000 period shows an equally dramatic average increase of 0.358. When we used expenditure, rather than log-expenditure, we observed a less notable reduction in the intermediate period, as well as a milder increase in the last period. This suggests more variation among the relatively lower expenditure groups.

15. The data show strong upward positional mobility in Peru for the bottom quintiles and a relative deterioration for the middle quintiles. In part this movement reflects the benefits that stabilization had for the poor, who were least able to protect themselves from the negative effects of hyperinflation in the late 1980s, as well as changes in opportunity generated by positive rates of growth following stabilization—the highest rate in the world (14 percent in 1994) for one year of the period. It may also reflect the government's efforts to redirect public expenditures to the poorest groups.

5 percent and 1 percent, respectively. Alternatively, 11 percent of Peruvians that began in the fourth quintile fell all the way to the bottom, while only 5 percent of Americans experienced a similar drop.[16]

For Russia, we have data from a household survey, the Russia Longitudinal Monitoring Survey, or RLMS, for 1995–98, a period of extensive macroeconomic volatility. The survey covers approximately 6,000 households a year, and includes questions, similar to those in the Peruvian and U.S. surveys, about subjective well-being and perceptions of past progress in addition to objective income data. From the survey data we were able to construct a longitudinal (panel) sample of approximately 2,000 households.[17] In terms of objective mobility, Russian households experienced extensive movements both up and down the income ladder, although downward trends were more dominant in Russia than in Peru. Mean incomes went down for all groups over the period by an average of 17.2 percent. In terms of positional movement, 48 percent of those in the fourth quintile experienced downward mobility, with 11 percent ending up in the bottom quintile and 15 percent in the second quintile (table 3-4). Of those in Russia who started the period in the top income quintile, only 40 percent retained their position, and 9 percent fell to the bottom income quintile; in Peru 3 percent of those at the top fell to the very bottom.[18]

For South Africa, a study of panel data covering 1993 through 1998 examines transitions in and out of poverty.[19] The study finds that 66 percent of those below the poverty line in 1993 were still there in 1998, while 57 percent

16. Mishel, Bernstein, and Schmitt (1999). Note that these data compare expenditure data for Peru with income data for the United States. In general, expenditure varies much less than income and thus the Peru matrix actually *understates* the amount of mobility. The data for the two countries are more comparable than they might at first appear, however, because the U.S. data have been smoothed to account for short-term fluctuations; that is, three years of income have been averaged for each period (1978–80 for the 1979 figure and 1988–90 for the 1989 figure). Another way of looking at this comparison is to find the period in the U.S. data where the mobility flows are the same in magnitude as Peru's. We had to look at a 24-year period (1969–94) of U.S. data to find mobility flows that matched those in Peru during the 9-year period.

17. The survey, the Russia Longitudinal Monitoring Survey, has been conducted in Russia since 1995 by the Russian Institute of Nutrition, the University of North Carolina at Chapel Hill, and the Institute of Sociology of the Russian Academy of Sciences, with support from the World Bank, the U.S. Agency for International Development, and the National Science Foundation, among others.

18. Our calculations based on RLMS data.

19. Carter and May (1999).

Table 3-4. *Relative Mobility in Russia, 1995–1998*[a]

Percent

Quintile 1991	Quintile 2000					
	1	2	3	4	5	Total
1	39	26	16	10	9	100
2	25	28	22	16	10	100
3	16	21	25	22	16	100
4	11	15	22	26	26	100
5	9	10	16	26	40	100
Total	100	100	100	100	100	100

Source: Authors' calculations from Russia Longitudinal Monitoring Surveys (1998–99).
a. Quintiles are calculated using equivalence income.

of those who were in the highest income category were still there in 1998 (this category covered people whose incomes were 2.5 times that of the poverty line or more). Only 3 percent of those who were below the poverty line in 1993 reached the highest income category by 1998. (See table 3-5; note that this table depicts absolute movements in and out of poverty, rather than positional shifts across quintiles.)

The data, and the authors' analysis, suggest that a significant proportion of poverty in South Africa is more chronic or permanent than it is in Peru, Russia, or the United States. With the exception of a few cases in the sample that experienced unexpected exogenous shocks (luck), moving out of poverty for South Africans was directly linked to the ownership of productive assets, such as land, education, or surplus household labor. This is in

Table 3-5. *Absolute Mobility in South Africa, 1993–1998*[a]

Expenditure class 1993	Expenditure class 1998						
	<0.5PL	<PL	<1.25PL	<1.5PL	<2.5PL	>2.5PL	Total
<0.5PL	17	49	8	8	17	3	100
<PL	18	49	9	6	17	3	100
<1.25PL	9	40	13	8	21	8	100
<1.5PL	8	39	11	11	20	12	100
<2.5PL	5	19	14	9	29	25	100
>2.5PL	2	6	7	5	23	57	100

Source: Carter and May (1999).
a. Expenditure classes are indicated by top poverty line (PL) boundaries.

keeping with cross-country studies that find that the ownership of assets reduces the risk of households' falling into poverty as a result of macroeconomic volatility.[20]

An obvious related question is the extent to which the probability of being chronically poor is transmitted intergenerationally. We were unable to answer this question because of the short-term nature of our panel data. It is plausible that all countries have some intergenerational poverty, but that the degree varies among them, depending in part on the general level of income mobility, and in part on other factors, such as social structure, racial barriers, access to education and other services, and so on.

In the absence of panel data, meanwhile, it is possible to infer trends in mobility with proxy panel data, either by matching cohorts across household surveys or through recall data (which has obvious problems). These proxy data permit a better—if incomplete—picture of the intergenerational component. Nancy Birdsall, Jere Behrman, and Miguel Székely have constructed indexes of intergenerational mobility using twenty-eight household surveys in sixteen countries of Latin America, taken between 1980 and 1996, to explore the effects of economic policies, macroeconomic conditions, and education programs on that mobility. They calculate the schooling gap per child as the expected years of schooling—that is, the number of years of schooling that child would have been expected to complete had she or he entered school at age 6 and advanced one grade each year—minus the number of years the child had actually completed at the time of the survey. They consider schooling gaps separately for four age groups: 10–12, 13–15, 16–18, and 19–21 years, as family background is more likely to matter more for older children. They then calculate family background by dividing households in the sample into five quintiles, according to parental schooling.

Their results confirm for a large number of countries over many years that family background has a significant association with length of children's schooling. As expected, children of higher-income and better-educated parents everywhere and at all times are likely to do better. But their results also suggest that the implied link is subject to substantial variation across countries and periods, depending on macroeconomic conditions and public policy in education. They find that the depth of financial markets and public

20. De Ferranti and others (2000).

policies that emphasize public spending on basic schooling enhance inter-generational mobility.[21] Although the immediate effects of market and education policy reforms on current income distribution are not evident, longer-run positive effects of greater mobility on distribution seem plausible.

In a similar effort to measure trends in social mobility, which broadly defined includes income, expenditure, occupational, and other measures of mobility, Dahan and Gaviria construct an index of mobility based on the correlation of schooling gaps between siblings: the between-family variance of mean schooling gaps versus the overall variance of the gaps.[22] With perfect mobility, family background would not matter, and siblings would be no more alike than any two people taken at random (barring shared genetic traits). In an immobile society, family backgrounds would dominate, and most siblings would fare alike. Dahan and Gaviria compute their index based on household surveys from sixteen Latin American countries and find that social mobility is highly correlated with both average schooling and inequality of schooling. They also find a strong relationship between mobility and education expenditures, and only weak relationships between mobility and gross domestic product per capita and mobility and income distribution.[23] More generally, they find that most countries in the region, with the exception of Mexico, experienced a slight increase in mobility in the early 1980s and mid-1990s.

Hojman, in a study on Chile, focuses on "market-driven, medium-term mobility": changes in mobility trends that are driven by policy change.[24] After two decades of structural reforms, Chile's highly unequal income distribution remains very similar to the period before reforms, despite major strides in reducing absolute poverty. In a study of trends in Chile's wage rates (based on occupational categories) from 1986 to 1992, Hojman finds that although absolute income increased across the board, by far the largest relative increases went to managerial (skilled) personnel. Their gains increased

21. In contrast, expenditures on higher education were inversely related to enhanced inter-generational mobility, because higher education expenditures in Latin America overwhelmingly favor the highest income deciles. See Behrman, Birdsall, and Székely (2000b).

22. Dahan and Gaviria (1999). For a similar approach and findings for Brazil, see Lam and Schoeni (1993).

23. The authors do find a high correlation between inequality and assortative mating in the region. This is in keeping with the findings by Burtless (1999) pointing to changing family composition as one of the key explanatory variables for increasing inequality in the United States.

24. Hojman (2000).

from 419 percent of average earnings to 515 percent of the average by 1992, while unskilled workers remained at about 50 percent of the average throughout the period. These findings are also supported by evidence from annual, regionwide cross sections, which suggest that the rewards to skilled labor have far outpaced those to unskilled labor. The explanation for these trends is twofold. First, trade liberalization has rewarded skilled, rather than unskilled, labor in the region, contrary to the predictions of classic economic theory.[25] Second, because education policy has not kept up with demand in the region, the relative scarcity of skilled labor has further increased its marginal gains relative to those of unskilled labor.

Terrell examines changes in relative earnings and employment status of workers in the post-communist economies.[26] She finds that the winners so far have been young, educated men whose skills enable them to exploit new opportunities in the private sector. The growth in women's returns to education has lagged behind men's, and the skills of older workers are much less valued than they were before the transition. In contrast to Latin America, the much more dramatic changes in the structure of economies and welfare systems in Eastern Europe and Russia have led to significant downward mobility. At the same time, many educated groups, whose labor was undervalued under state planning, have experienced upward mobility.

What Explains Patterns in Mobility?

These studies suggest that mobility rates vary across countries and that they can also change quite substantially over time within countries. In many countries the poor do indeed move out of poverty, but at the same time substantial numbers of people fall from the middle of the distribution into poverty. What explains these movements?

Education, Assets, and Incentives

Several variables influence an individual's chance of moving out of or falling into poverty. The most commonly cited variables, and perhaps the most

25. For a discussion of the effects of trade opening on differential rewards to labor, see Robbins (1996). For a discussion of empirical evidence of differential returns to labor in Latin America, see Lora and Londoño (1998). See also Londoño, Spilimbergo, and Székely (1997).
26. Terrell (2000). For a discussion of changes in occupational mobility, see Mateju (2000).

consistent from country to country and over time, are sociodemographic determinants. Family background matters. Children of wealthier and more educated parents do better across the board, regardless of the particular country and policy contexts, unless there are extreme circumstances, such as severe hyperinflation.[27]

In Latin America, for example, a strong correlation occurs between the distribution of income and the distribution of education of the heads and the members of households of employed workers. The higher the educational level of workers, the higher their income levels. And the performance of children is clearly segmented, depending on the income levels of their parents. Whereas children from low-income households had an average of 46.0 percent on a fourth grade performance test, those in medium-income households had an average score of 54.1 percent and those from high-income families had an average of 65.5 percent. These differences in test performance are directly reflected in higher levels of repetition in primary school for those in the lowest-income stratum, as well as more interruptions and delays in completing primary school.[28] In addition, the link between parents' educational attainment and their children's seems to be very strong and even stronger where public school systems are weak.[29]

Educational performance, not surprisingly, also has effects on future prospects of moving out of poverty. On average a person in Latin America needs ten or eleven years of formal schooling to have a 90 percent or higher probability of not falling into poverty (or of moving out of poverty). Just two fewer years of schooling results in a 20 percent drop in income for the rest of the person's active life.[30]

Studies of panel data for rural El Salvador (1995–97) and metropolitan Brazil (1982–1999) support these regionwide statistics.[31] In El Salvador, the

27. Under extreme circumstances such as hyperinflation, even the rewards to education can be severely eroded. Using panel data from Peru for 1985 through 1990, Glewwe and Hall (1998) find that during the crisis and hyperinflation years, even higher education was insufficient to prevent individuals from falling into poverty. The one variable that did consistently provide such protection was access to transfers from abroad.

28. ECLAC (2000).

29. For Latin America, see Behrman, Birdsall, and Székely (2000b). According to Mc-Murrer and Sawhill (1998), the importance of family background matters less for mobility in the United States than it used to, but access to good quality higher education matters more. And access to good quality education is in turn strongly linked to parental income levels.

30. ECLAC (2000).

31. De Ferranti and others (2000).

years of schooling attained by the household head have strong and signifi-cant effects on income. In Brazil, more years of schooling were associated with a smaller probability of transition into poverty and a larger transition rate out of poverty, both during recessions and growth spurts.[32]

The relevant question for public policy is the extent to which the influ-ences of family background can be mediated and the playing field leveled. Although it is unlikely that policy will ever be able to achieve a mobility transition matrix that reflects a Rawlsian distribution of opportunity, pol-icy should be able to prevent societies from falling into the situation shown in table 3-1A, where there is no mobility at all and parents' backgrounds completely determine their children's fates (this can be said if $T_1 - T_0 \geq$ 30 years, or if T_0 = parents' y, T_1 = children's y).

Education matters a great deal in virtually all contexts—although differ-ent levels of education can produce differences in marginal rewards—and it is an obvious focus for public policy. Several studies also show that having some stock of assets also matters, both in protecting individuals from downward mobility and in permitting them to make productive invest-ments in human and physical capital.[33]

Although education and assets are extremely important, they are not the only factors determining intra- and intergenerational mobility. Rigid social structures, racial and gender discrimination, unequal access to political rights and to health care and other critical services could all limit or even block the upward mobility of disadvantaged groups. A full discussion of such factors is beyond the scope of this chapter, but it is important to note their existence in many societies, both developed and developing.

Finally, the structure of incentives also matters. If rewards to labor are extremely low, for example, poor parents will have low incentives to save and invest in their children's education. Birdsall, Pinkney, and Sabot attribute higher-level savings and growth in East Asia than in Latin America

32. Results for a panel in metropolitan Mexico (1994–97) were more mixed, as households headed by college-educated males suffered larger proportionate falls in income as a consequence of the 1995 crisis than did those with primary or secondary education. When coping variables were included in the regressions, however, defined namely as entry into the labor force of an additional family member, the advantage of the less educated became insignificant. These results echo those of Herrera (1999), who finds that household heads with secondary education in urban Peru had a lower probability of exiting poverty than did those with either primary or higher education. To some extent, these results may stem from trade and technology-driven changes in the global economy, which are changing the rewards to different levels of education.

33. De Ferranti and others (2000); Carter and May (1999).

to a labor-intensive growth model used in East Asia, which gave the poor incentives to invest in their children's education. Latin America, in contrast, relied on a capital-intensive growth model with low returns to labor, which discouraged education investments by the poor.[34] Similarly, tax structures matter. The myth (if not the reality) of the United States having higher mobility rates than Europe is based in large part on a less onerous tax regime in the former, making rags to riches stories more possible.[35]

Market Failures and Government Failures

Yet in many countries, particularly developing economies, certain market and government failures can introduce perverse incentives or block the ability of the poor to accumulate education and other productive assets. Inequality in some instances acts as a distortion. Sheahan and Iglesias distinguish between constructive inequality, which rewards productivity and innovation, and destructive inequality, which blocks the productive potential of the poor.[36] A wide body of research suggests that high inequality and low growth in Latin America both reflect and reinforce the lack of productive opportunities for the poor, the second kind of inequality.[37]

In economies where opportunities are limited to those with privileged access to education and credit, among other key productive assets, the poor have neither the capacity nor the incentive to make human capital investments.[38] In part, and particularly for the very poor, this lack of capacity stems from sheer inadequacy of income and assets. Yet it also stems from the negative incentives and low expectations that result from persistent and high levels of inequality. Without human capital, the poor, in a vicious circle, stay poor, and as their productive potential is squandered, overall economic growth suffers.[39]

---

34. Birdsall, Pinkney, and Sabot (1999).

35. See, among others, Solon (1992); McMurrer and Sawhill (1998). Several sociological studies, meanwhile, compare mobility rates between the United States and Europe in the past few decades and find no significant difference between the two. See, for example, Erikson and Goldthorpe (1985).

36. Sheahan and Iglesias (1998).

37. See, for example, Birdsall, Ross, and Sabot (1995).

38. Much of the literature describing the effects of human capital investments on growth focuses primarily or solely on the effects of education. Here we define human capital broadly, to include investments in education, health, and occupational skills.

39. For a detailed description of how asset inequality has constrained growth in the region, see Birdsall and Londoño (1997).

A common assumption is that market reforms are bad for the poor. Although the effects of market reforms on inequality are unclear at best and the subject of a great deal of debate, the positive effects of such reforms on the poor are quite clear.[40] The elimination of high levels of inflation, for example, has important and positive effects for the poor, who are least able to protect themselves from its costs. During periods of high inflation, wealthier individuals can protect themselves through mechanisms such as indexed banking accounts and transferring assets abroad, things that the poor are rarely able to do. And the elimination of market distortions can be critical to opening new opportunities for the poor.

In contrast, interventions designed specifically to help the poor with redistributive transfers often have perverse outcomes, such as the capture of the subsidies by the nonpoor. Market reforms emphasize productivity-enhancing measures that are sustainable in fiscal terms and avoid the kinds of disincentives at the microeconomic level that create dependence or disrupt the autonomous efforts and coping strategies of the poor.[41] The emphasis is on introducing incentives that encourage the poor to invest in human capital and to contribute to, as well as benefit from, the growth process, providing them with new opportunities for upward mobility.

The elimination of distortions can also foster the potential of the private sector to provide such opportunities. In Mexico, for example, a country that has made a great deal of progress implementing market reforms, the private sector created more than 12 million new jobs between 1987 and 1998, while the public sector created 143,000 jobs, a ratio of 87 to 1. In contrast, in several countries that have made less progress implementing reforms, such as Gabon, Guatemala, Kenya, and Uruguay, that ratio is less than 15 to 1.[42] A recent survey in Venezuela showed that finding a job was the single most important factor in explaining transitions out of poverty. The sources of new jobs for those that escaped poverty were the public sector (11 percent), the formal private sector (31 percent), and the informal private sector (58 percent).[43]

---

40. See Birdsall, Graham, and Sabot (1998). For empirical evidence, see Londoño and Székely (1997). Morley (1994) hints at the beginnings of this trend. Others, such as Berry (1996), do not agree that these positive trends are present.

41. For a review of such strategies see Graham (1994).

42. International Finance Corporation (2000).

43. International Finance Corporation (2000).

It is fairly evident that the transition to a market economy and to global integration can create new opportunities for the poor. Yet it also introduces new vulnerabilities. These vulnerabilities are linked both to the availability of adequate safety nets and to individuals' ability to participate in a global economy that increasingly rewards those with skills and education. Removing market distortions is, without a doubt, a necessary step to creating new opportunities for the poor to move out of poverty. It is not, however, a sufficient one.

Winners and Losers in a Technology-Based Economy

To get ahead in today's globalized, technology-driven economy, a person needs not just education, but higher levels of education. Increasingly, a secondary education is insufficient to guarantee a decent—and stable—standard of living. The wage premium for skilled, educated workers is rising, a result of some combination of technological change biased toward skill and trade-induced changes in demand for skills.[44] In Latin America, for example, the differential between the incomes of professionals and technicians and those of wage earners in low-productivity sectors swelled by 28 percent, on average, between 1990 and 1997.[45]

Directly related to this, the single most important characteristic defining the wealthiest households in Latin America (those in the very top of the tenth decile) is that most adults in those households have at least some university education.[46] In Brazil, for example, the average 25-year-old in the tenth, or highest, decile (of the distribution defined in terms of household income per capita) has eleven years of education; the average in the ninth decile is only eight years (implying that many 25-year-olds in this decile

---

44. On the United States, see Burtless (1999). On Latin America, see Duryea and Székely (1999).

45. ECLAC (2000).

46. Inter-American Development Bank (1998). A recent study of Latin American households finds that the profile of the average individual in the top 10 percent of the distribution is closer to the prototype of a highly educated professional earning labor income than it is to that of a capital owner living on profits. Although this finding does not imply that Latin American inequality is not driven by a small number of individuals at the top of the distribution earning profits from capital investments (particularly as household surveys do not document this type of income very accurately), it does suggest the extent to which skilled labor has gained relative to other groups. See Székely and Hilgert (1999).

have not attended secondary school); and the average in the middle two deciles is not even five years.[47] On average the ratio between mean schooling of 25-year-olds in the top decile and those in the middle is 2 to 1. The difference in the United States is much smaller: adults in the top decile have only 1.2 times the mean number of school years as those in the middle deciles.[48]

These trends in education illustrate a more general point. Wherever there is a history of low enrollment, recent increases in enrollment will increase inequality in the distribution of education. If demand for the relatively skilled increases faster than supply, those with scarce skills will enjoy increasing returns to those skills in the labor market. Latin America is an extreme example. Within Latin America, however, even a country like Costa Rica, with a longer and deeper history of widespread education, has nearly a 2:1 ratio between the education of adults in the top decile and those in the middle deciles.

Education: The Reference Bar Shifts Upward

Figures 3-2a and 3-2b illustrate that during the 1990s, returns to higher education in Latin America rose dramatically relative to returns to secondary and primary education.[49] They also show a general trend of decreasing relative marginal returns to secondary education. It seems the reference bar has shifted upward.[50] In the 1960s and 1970s a secondary education was sufficient to attain a stable job and a "middle-class"—indeed, a fairly privileged—

47. Inter-American Development Bank (1998: appendix table 1.2.III).

48. For this comparison we use household survey data for Latin America and the *Current Population Survey* (CPS), March Supplement, 1998, for the United States. Data here refer to all adults; the difference in the ratios would be greater for 25-year-olds, because education levels have increased substantially in Latin America in recent decades. Data from the CPS are calculated after constructing an equivalence scale for educational attainment categories (below 9th grade = 6 years; 9th to 12th grade = 10.5; high-school = 12; some college = 14; B.A. = 16; M.A. = 18; professional degree = 19; Ph.D. = 24).

49. On changes in returns to education in Latin America, see Duryea and Székely (1998); Behrman, Birdsall, and Székely (2000b). Differentials in returns to education are also rising in Eastern Europe; see Rutkowski (1999); Terrell (2000); Vecernik (1996).

50. This shifting of the reference bar is probably based on the nature of education as well as its level, with most students in the region attaining the kind of skills necessary to participate in the new technology economy in university or in postsecondary vocational education, rather than in secondary school. We are grateful to Selim Jahan for pointing out the distinct effects of the nature and level of education.

Figure 3-2. *Latin America in the 1990s*

A. Marginal returns to education

Marginal return to completing a level of education

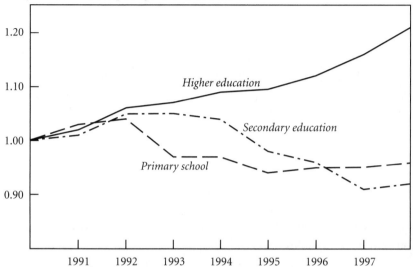

B. Wage differentials by level of education

Relative log wage

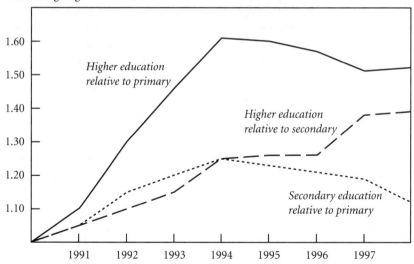

Source: Behrman, Birdsall, and Székely (2000a).

standard of living. But by the 1990s it neither guaranteed a well-paying job nor protected its possessor from falling into poverty. As explained more fully later, many of those who had finished secondary school but had not gone on to higher levels of education were public sector workers; as the 1990s progressed, there were far fewer public sector jobs, and they were also less desirable.[51]

A recent study on intergenerational mobility in Brazil is consistent with these findings of relative losses among secondary school graduates. The study suggests that workers in 1973 were much better off than their parents, almost independently of their education. In the 1970s a new working urban class was benefiting from rapid growth. In contrast, Brazilian workers in 1996 were only better off than their parents to the extent that their educational level had increased substantially. In the early stages of industrialization, mobility was structural in nature: opportunities were created by a fast-growing economy. More recently, mobility had become more circular, a consequence of more competitive labor markets and larger wage gaps based on education and skills.[52]

Findings from an anthropological study of households in three Rio de Janeiro shantytowns, surveyed in 1968 and revisited in 1999, support the same conclusion.[53] Most parents felt that their children had a better life than they did because the children had more education and a higher standard of living. Yet children's responses demonstrated substantial frustration because, despite higher levels of education and access to consumer goods, they were unable to break out of their parents' occupational categories. In most cases, changing occupational categories requires obtaining a university education, an objective that eludes most low-income Brazilians.

If the technology-driven economy has rewarded those with skills in Latin America, how have those without skills fared? The poor, for the most part, have benefited from the reduction in high levels of inflation, the removal of a number of market distortions, and the restoration of economic growth.[54] They have also benefited, at least in some countries, from

51. Finally, as discussed earlier, where the levels of macroeconomic volatility are extreme, even education may be an insufficient buffer from significant downward mobility.

52. Pastore and do Valle Silva (2000).

53. The 1999 survey was a pilot in which only a subsample of the original 200 households were interviewed. See Perlman (1999).

54. See, among others, Bruno, Ravallion, and Squire (1996). Dollar and Kray (2000), meanwhile, show that the poor—defined as the bottom quintile of the population across

a reorientation of public expenditures in their direction, as the focus shifted from universally available public services to targeted programs for the lowest-income households.

The effort to ensure that public expenditures reach the poor is important. But in countries where the shift has provided very clear benefits for the poor—as in Chile and Peru—it has come as much, if not more, at the expense of middle-income households as of wealthy ones. That is because increased expenditures on programs for the poor have been financed largely by value added taxes, which are not progressive, or by a reallocation of existing expenditures.[55] Wherever the wealthy do not rely on public services, such as transportation and emergency hospital care—which is the case in many countries in the developing world—reductions in quality and coverage of services have a stronger impact on middle-income groups who were previously the main beneficiaries of public social spending.[56] In countries such as Brazil, the Czech Republic, Egypt, and Mexico, for example, the middle class was the main beneficiary of spending on secondary and higher education programs. It thus was most affected when these and other services deteriorated in quality as public funding failed to keep up with enlarged programs or the focus of expenditures shifted to targeted programs.

Another trend related to the new economy, which has also had mixed effects on the poor and the middle class, is the reduction of public sector employment. White-collar occupations, for which a secondary education was sufficient and which guaranteed a "middle-class" standard of living for large numbers of people in most developing economies, were found primarily in the public and parastatal sectors. Many developing countries have trimmed their public sector in order to achieve fiscally sustainable growth and remain competitive at an international level. Reductions in the size of the civil service and privatization of state-owned enterprises resulted in the

---

countries—benefit as much as other groups do. At the same time, they are the least able to use the usual means, including bribes, international bank accounts, and political clout, to negotiate market distortions.

55. For Chile, Cowan and de Gregorio (2000), show income gains attributable to public social spending of 39 and 28 percent for the two poorest quintiles, compared to 20 and 10 percent for the third and fourth quintiles. For a summary of the targeting approach and its effects, see van de Walle and Nead (1995).

56. For detail, see Graham (1998).

Figure 3-3. *Public Sector Employment Share Levels, Selected Countries, 1980s and 1990s*

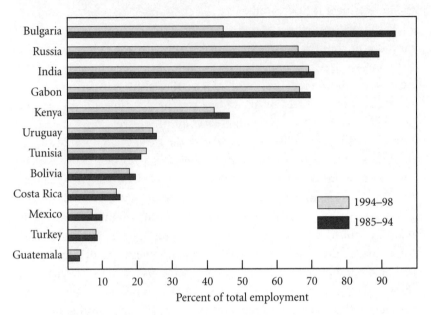

Source: Authors' calculations, based on data provided by Guy Pfeffermann, chief economist, International Finance Corporation, 2000.

elimination of millions of secure jobs during the 1990s. Figure 3-3 suggests that since 1985 the percentage of workers employed in public sector jobs has been decreasing for most countries. Not surprisingly, transitional econo- mies (in our sample for figure 3-3, Bulgaria and Russia) had the highest ini- tial levels as well as the most dramatic decline. With the exception of Tunisia and Guatemala, all the countries in the sample show decreasing shares in public sector employment.[57]

Other evidence from Latin America indicates that increases in private sector jobs have not fully compensated for the loss of secure jobs in govern- ment and state-owned enterprises. Unemployment rates were higher in the mid-1990s than they were in the early 1990s in most countries (the excep- tions are in Central America, where the *maquila* industries have grown, and

57. The authors are grateful to Guy Pfeffermann of the International Finance Corporation for providing these data.

in Bolivia and Peru).[58] Even those public sector workers who kept their jobs probably lost ground in relative terms. In Peru gains in income in the period 1989–96 were three times greater for private than for public sector workers.[59]

In addition, data gathered by the International Labor Organization show an increase in "unprotected" jobs in the ten countries with comparable figures covering the last decade or so.[60] Unprotected jobs are those in which workers have no written contract or social benefits. The increases do not necessarily imply that workers are worse off—they may receive higher hourly wages. They do imply, however, that workers enjoy less security. In Latin America the decline in protected jobs has probably affected middle-income workers more than poor workers, because workers in poor households were rarely among those protected in the first place. The combination of declining numbers of public sector jobs and fewer protected jobs has led to a shrinking in the size and income share of the middle class in many countries.[61]

Middle Income Stress and Top-Driven Inequality

In a recent paper, Birdsall, Graham, and Pettinato develop an income-based measure of the middle class, defined as the population sector with incomes between 75 percent and 125 percent of the median income.[62] This income-based measure is distinct from the usual class- or occupation-based measure relied on by sociologists, which literally captures the middle stratum in income terms. With this income-based measure, Birdsall, Graham, and Pettinato can compare the size of the middle class across countries and

58. Rodrik (1999), citing Inter-American Development Bank data.
59. Authors' calculations based on data for Lima, cited by Saavedra (1998).
60. Rodrik (1999) compiled the ILO data.
61. Even in the United States, traditionally known as the land of mobility and opportunity, more people are moving out of the middle class—into higher or lower income categories—than into it, at least as shown by a study of transitions into and out of the "middle class" by Duncan, Smeeding, and Rogers (1993). Using absolute level thresholds based on common income-to-needs ratios—the ratio between the household income and the poverty line—they conclude that the U.S. middle class shrank in the 1980s and the beginning of the 1990s. The thresholds for the definition of the middle strata are constructed using arbitrary ratios between income levels and the poverty line. They also report that in the 1980s correspondingly fewer poor families moved up or rich families down into the middle groups than in previous decades.
62. See Birdsall, Graham, and Pettinato (2000).

within countries over time, at least for those countries where comparable household level income data are available. This measure also allows comparisons of absolute income levels of the middle class across countries.

The middle group's share in total population depends on the extent to which the tails of the income distribution are large relative to the middle. The group's share of income does not necessarily correspond to its share of the total population. Nor are the households in this group necessarily households of "average" per capita income; in countries with a high share of households below a poverty line and a highly skewed distribution at the top, middle-class households typically have income below the average and may even include some households defined by the particular country as "poor."[63] This is the case in Latin America, where the distribution of income is highly concentrated at the top and where the difference between mean and median income is so great that even the most well-off of the middle group of households have income far below the average. But even in high-income countries, most households in this middle group have below-average income.[64]

Table 3-6 demonstrates how the middle strata compare across countries using information on income from the most recent available household survey for each country.[65] The share of population is lowest, at about 22 percent, in Latin America and highest, at about 42 percent, in the transitional economies. The share of income, given population, is systematically lower in Latin America. Table 3-7 shows per capita gross national product (GNP), average household per capita income, and the absolute income range of the group in the middle.[66] The income of a "middle"-income individual in

63. This is not the case for any country for which we have data (see table 3-7), but it could apply to countries in South Asia and Africa, using our definition.

64. Another finding from table 3-7 is the large difference between the figures for per capita gross national product, obtained at the aggregate level, and those for average income. Calculated from household surveys, average incomes are consistently smaller than per capita GNP, by an average ratio of 1:1.7. This has been observed also in the past and is a consequence of the differences in the definition of *product* and *income*. A large amount of this discrepancy is unexplained, even though corporate earnings may play an important role.

65. With the possible exceptions of Russia and the United States, these surveys are reasonably comparable across countries; the income variable has been constructed the same way from household survey information.

66. We use purchasing power parity to measure income, a procedure that minimizes differences between rich and poor countries because it corrects for the lower costs of nontradables in the poor countries.

Table 3-6. *The Size of the Middle Strata*

Percent (unless otherwise noted)

Country	Year	Middle class Population	Income	Ratio of income to population
High income		*37.2*	*31.6*	*0.85*
Australia	1994	28.6	23.5	0.82
Austria	1987	46.3	43.6	0.94
Belgium	1992	45.7	42.6	0.93
Canada	1994	36.0	31.8	0.88
Denmark	1992	46.5	41.3	0.89
Finland	1995	49.1	39.4	0.80
France	1994	36.6	30.6	0.84
Germany	1994	38.8	36.2	0.93
Ireland	1987	36.1	28.1	0.78
Israel	1992	30.3	23.7	0.78
Italy	1995	32.5	26.5	0.82
Luxembourg	1994	41.3	36.8	0.89
Netherlands	1994	36.6	30.8	0.84
Spain	1990	36.0	30.0	0.83
Sweden	1995	38.0	31.6	0.83
Switzerland	1992	34.5	31.4	0.91
Taiwan	1995	36.6	28.8	0.79
United Kingdom	1995	33.1	26.0	0.79
United States	1999	24.2	17.6	0.73
Transition economies		*41.7*	*34.5*	*0.83*
Czech Republic	1992	60.6	54.7	0.90
Hungary	1994	43.8	35.0	0.80
Poland	1995	36.0	31.6	0.88
Russian Federation	1997	28.6	16.9	0.59
Slovak Republic	1992	58.2	54.6	0.94
Latin America		*21.7*	*13.2*	*0.61*
Brazil	1996	20.7	9.6	0.46
Chile	1996	21.5	14.2	0.66
Costa Rica	1997	24.5	17.6	0.72
Mexico	1996	22.4	13.5	0.60
Panama	1995	19.4	11.4	0.59
Peru	1997	21.4	13.1	0.61

Source: Birdsall, Graham, and Pettinato (2000).

Table 3-7. *Income Levels and Ranges of the Middle Strata*
Dollars

Country	Year	GNP per capita	Average income	Middle-strata income thresholds[a]	
				Bottom	Top
High income		*18,775*	*10,909*	*6,935*	*11,558*
Australia	1994	18,210	10,264	6,282	10,470
Austria	1987	14,880	8,644	5,941	9,902
Belgium	1992	19,970	9,161	6,251	10,418
Canada	1994	20,190	13,671	8,684	14,474
Denmark	1992	19,300	10,369	7,076	11,794
Finland	1995	18,510	10,129	6,760	11,267
France	1994	20,310	11,704	7,279	12,132
Germany	1994	19,710	11,024	7,202	12,004
Ireland	1987	8,850	3,332	2,939	4,899
Israel	1992	14,530	8,608	5,065	8,445
Italy	1995	19,590	9,047	5,692	9,488
Luxembourg	1994	27,990	15,097	9,870	16,450
Netherlands	1994	19,050	10,284	6,553	10,921
Spain	1990	12,220	5,707	3,548	5,913
Sweden	1995	18,500	10,454	7,483	12,472
Switzerland	1992	23,540	15,980	10,149	16,916
Taiwan	1995	12,838	8,587	5,296	8,826
United Kingdom	1995	19,450	11,739	6,989	11,648
United States	1999	29,080	23,478	12,699	21,165
Transition economies		*5,555*	*3,632*	*2,732*	*4,552*
Czech Republic	1992	8,590	3,701	2,520	4,200
Hungary	1994	6,190	2,797	1,779	2,965
Poland	1995	5,700	3,082	1,942	3,237
Russian Federation	1997	4,280	5,978	5,309	8,849
Slovak Republic	1992	6,050	2,672	1,897	3,156
Latin America		*7,200*	*4,697*	*1,649*	*2,748*
Brazil	1996	6,250	4,563	1,326	2,211
Chile	1996	11,620	8,803	3,016	5,027
Costa Rica	1997	6,510	4,326	1,926	3,210
Mexico	1996	7,660	2,883	1,000	1,666
Panama	1995	6,580	5,373	1,718	2,864
Peru	1997	4,580	2,232	908	1,513

Source: Birdsall, Graham, and Pettinato (2000).

a. Local currency figures converted into "international U.S. dollars," using PPP conversion rates available from the World Bank, for the most recent year available.

low-income Brazil, for example, is obviously lower in absolute terms than that of one in Taiwan.

Birdsall, Graham, and Pettinato developed a new measure—which they call middle-income stress, or MIS—designed to capture the income difference between the top of the distribution and the middle.[67] The measure compares the median income of the population that generates the top 50 percent of total income to the median income for the total population. The authors theorize that stress increases as the gap increases between the median income for the total population and the median income of the top 50 percent.

Another new measure, Wolfson's polarization index, captures the extent to which the distribution is concentrating at the tails and thinning out at the middle, with a focus on the share of the bottom half. The Gini, for example, would not capture the difference in a society of three individuals where income was distributed from top to bottom as 9 - 5 - 1 compared with one where income was distributed: 9 - 4 - 2. Although total income is the same in either case, the Gini would indicate a better distribution in the first society. In contrast the ratio of the ninetieth percentile to the median would suggest the reverse.[68] Wolfson's measure would rate the latter distribution better. Indeed, changes in both the MIS and the polarization index do not always run in the same direction as changes in the Gini. [69]

From the mid-1980s to the late 1990s, inequality as measured by the Gini increased for the former communist countries, particularly for Russia. In contrast, it decreased slightly for Latin American countries that adopted strong market reforms. Middle-income stress also fell slightly for most, although not all, of the strong market reformers in Latin America, while polarization displayed more mixed trends. In Russia, where reforms were far less complete, as well as in several other transition economies, increases in both polarization and MIS were significant (table 3-8).[70]

---

67. Birdsall, Graham, and Pettinato (2000).

68. Wolfson (1997).Wolfson's measure is computed as $W = [2(2T - Gini)] / Mt$, where $T = 0.5 - L(0.5)$, with $L(0.5)$ = the income (y) share of the bottom 50 percent of the population, and Mt = median (y)/mean (y). The denominator is the inverse of a standard measure of inequality, the mean over the median, a ratio that increases as incomes at the top pull up the average relative to the median.

69. For detail, see Birdsall, Graham, and Pettinato (2000).

70. For detail on the limited nature of the reforms in Russia, see Gaddy and Ickes (1998).

Table 3-8. *Changes in Middle Income Stress and Inequality Measures*
Percent

Country	Period	MIS[a]	Polarization[b]	Inequality[c]
High income		*0.6*	*1.6*	*1.6*
Australia	1985–94	−2.6	4.4	2.4
Austria	1987	n.a.	n.a.	n.a.
Belgium	1985–92	−1.1	−3.1	−19.6
Canada	1987–94	−0.4	−2.9	−6.1
Denmark	1987–92	−4.8	−8.6	−10.2
Finland	1987–95	3.0	5.5	2.7
France	1989–94	3.7	3.1	5.9
Germany	1984–94	−3.7	3.9	1.8
Ireland	1987	n.a.	n.a.	n.a.
Israel	1986–92	1.0	2.3	−0.1
Italy	1986–95	0.1	7.7	7.5
Luxembourg	1985–94	3.0	1.3	26.4
Netherlands	1987–94	6.5	1.2	8.3
Spain	1980–90	−4.6	−5.7	−5.7
Sweden	1987–97	−3.1	4.7	−5.0
Switzerland	1982–92	−8.9	−5.9	−8.0
Taiwan*	1981–95	−0.6	−0.6	−0.6
United Kingdom	1986–95	14.3	13.0	21.2
United States	1992–99	8.9	7.0	6.1
Transition economies		*10.8*	*10.4*	*14.2*
Czech Republic	1992	n.a.	n.a.	n.a.
Hungary	1991–94	10.2	14.6	12.3
Poland	1986–95	8.8	22.5	19.0
Russian Federation	1992–95	5.9	−0.1	3.6
Russian Federation	1995–97	18.6	4.6	21.9
Slovak Republic	1992	n.a.	n.a.	n.a.
Latin America		*−11.4*	*−3.6*	*−4.7*
Brazil	1988–96	−15.2	−4.3	−4.9
Chile	1987–96	−23.3	−1.5	−5.0
Costa Rica	1991–97	0.3	−1.7	3.3
Mexico	1989–96	−3.5	−1.3	4.1
Panama	1991–95	0.2	−0.7	−3.9
Peru	1985–97	−27.2	−12.4	−21.9

Source: Birdsall, Graham, and Pettinato (2000).

n.a. Not available.

a. Middle-income stress, calculated as the ratio of the median income of the top 50 percent income households to the total median.

b. Wolfson coefficient.

c. Gini coefficient.

These shifts in the size and share of the middle class across countries and the limited data available on mobility trends in particular countries all suggest a great deal of movement up and down the income ladder driven at least in part by trends in the global economy. These trends are surely creating new opportunities for many people, but they are also creating insecurity for others, even those who are upwardly mobile. The changing nature of the social contract in many countries reinforces these stresses and insecurities.

Top-driven inequality exacerbates middle-income stress and more broadly spreads insecurities in general. Top-driven inequality is inequality that is driven by a skew at the top of the distribution, that is, high levels of wealth among those at the top of the distribution compared with the rest of society, where income is not that unequally distributed. In Latin America, for example, where inequality rates are especially top-heavy, a large gap appears between the top decile and the rest of the distribution, including the next wealthiest decile.[71]

Top-driven inequality results in part from the rising wage premium to skilled, educated workers, a trend discussed earlier. It may also result from a possible increase in wealth at the top, because more open capital markets enhance opportunities for high returns. In addition, taxes on mobile capital (to the extent they are effective) are probably declining, while in developing countries, shallow financial sectors and underdeveloped capital markets may be limiting investment opportunities for small savers and borrowers.[72] Yet because of the limited knowledge about these trends and for other reasons, top-driven inequality is difficult to measure.[73]

71. In many Latin American countries, the richest 10 percent earn three times the amount earned by the next richest 10 percent, whereas in Canada, the United Kingdom, and the United States, this difference does not exceed 1.6. If one compares points other than the top tail of the distribution for Latin America to other developed countries, meanwhile, the region has lower inequality than much more equal developed countries; see Székely and Hilgert (1999).

72. Tanzi (2000).

73. Several problems arise in measuring top-driven inequality. First, labor income is poorly measured at the top. For Latin America, Székely and Hilgert (1999) report that on average in the sixteen countries for which information is available, the total income of each of the ten richest households in the survey is very similar to the average wage of a middle manager. Studies of tax administration in developing countries also suggest substantial underreporting of labor income, often through extensive use of legal exemptions and deductions. Second, in all countries, income from wealth is undercounted, if counted at all. Third, typical measures of income distribution do not reflect changes in the income of middle-income households relative to high-income households. See Shome (1999); Tanzi and Zee (2000).

Nonetheless, the limited evidence about the effects of top-driven inequality is that it can reduce the subjective well-being of even those who are well off in absolute terms, but whose living standards are far from the highest income earners. Most of the literature, for example, finds that after a certain level of absolute income, individuals' subjective well-being is determined by relative rather than absolute income levels. These findings hold across countries, regions, and development levels, other than for the very poorest countries.[74] Concern for relative income differences can lead to an ever rising bar of perceived needs, as well as to conspicuous consumption or risky economic behavior, such as gambling, to demonstrate wealth or to make increases at the margin.[75]

Another trend, whose effects compound the contribution of top-driven inequality to insecurity and middle-income stress, is the widespread diffusion of information about consumer goods and consumption standards across countries and cultures. Before global economic integration began, the dividing line between the rich and the middle class was based on income standards *within* individual societies. Yet the spread of information and the opening of markets allowing imports of many more consumer goods have introduced absolute standards of consumption that cross national boundaries and are visible, if not attainable, for the majority of citizens in new market economies. Most citizens in these economies have access to television (and increasingly the Internet), and are deluged daily with advertisements for imported products, such as designer jeans, Nike shoes, and McDonald's hamburgers, as well as with television shows that depict lavish life-styles as the norm (even though most of them in reality are far from the average for the United States or any other industrialized economy). In the 1990s multinationals producing and exporting "global

74. Easterlin (1974) pioneered work in this area. Since then the general direction of his findings have been confirmed by several other authors, including Blanchflower and Oswald (1999) and Frey and Stutzer (1999). More recently, Graham and Pettinato (2001) found that similar determinants of subjective well-being, as well as similar concerns for relative income differences, held for a seventeen-country sample in Latin America.

75. Schor (1998) documents the effects of this rising consumption bar on consumers in the United States. Robson (1992) shows the effects of relative income differences on attitudes toward risk and consumption. Hojman (2000) shows how consumption driven by top-driven inequality leads to nonoptimal investments by the poor in Chile.

consumption goods" have significantly expanded their sales and operations in developing countries.[76]

Consumption standards are probably rising faster than average real incomes in many new market economies. Reaching the global standard is obviously much more difficult for middle-income households in a poor country than in a middle-income one. The absolute income differences *among* countries add to the pressures of relative income differences *within* countries.

A related development is the new international market for skilled labor. Young Ph.D.s and technocrats in many emerging market countries are often able to obtain jobs in finance or in universities in the developed countries at much higher salaries than those in similar sectors at home. Multinational companies, meanwhile, are increasingly outsourcing entire production lines to cities in new market economies, such as computer programming to New Delhi or state-of-the-art hardware manufacturing to San Jose, and pay wages that are typically higher than the average for the home country. As in the case of rising consumption standards, relative differences *within* countries become less important than absolute differences in skill and education levels *among* them in determining individuals' potential to participate in this sector of the globalized economy.

Summary of the Findings

Research findings suggest that opportunities and mobility are not allocated in a Rawlsian manner in the new market economies. An individual's place on the skill, education, and income ladder matters a great deal (both for the person and the person's children). Yet the findings also show that these societies are characterized by a remarkable degree of social mobility—both upward and downward—and low-income individuals have new opportunities to

---

76. This trend involves not only production—cheap labor—but more recently the exploitation of new consumer markets. Between 1995 and 1998, for example, Nike revenue grew by 82 percent in the United States, 119 percent in Europe, 144 percent in Asia and the Pacific, and 163 percent in Canada, Latin America, and the Caribbean. Between 1991 and 1996, the number of McDonald's restaurants increased by 60 percent in the industrial countries and by 307 percent in the developing countries. Data are from UNDP (1998) and Nike Inc.'s *Annual Report to the Securities and Exchange Commission,* filed in August 1998.

make substantial upward progress. The extent of movement up and down the income ladder in relatively short periods of time is precisely why we believe that a focus on mobility and opportunity is essential to complement traditional approaches to the measure of inequality.

New opportunities also come hand in hand with new vulnerabilities, which are the result of exogenously generated macroeconomic volatility, as well as of changes in the nature of both private and public sector employment opportunities. While opportunities for upward mobility may have increased for those at the bottom, the new vulnerabilities seem to affect particularly, but not exclusively, those in the middle stratum, many of whom suffer temporary spells of poverty. At the same time, the gains of those at the top of the income distribution have increased relative to the rest in many countries, and that contributes to both the perception and the reality that those in the middle are worse off, at least in relative terms.

Our review of winners and losers in the new global economy demonstrates the extent to which outcomes are influenced by contextual factors: the differential rewards that market policies have for various age, education, and skill cohorts; the role of relative income differences; and insecurity related to macroeconomic volatility and inadequate social insurance mechanisms. These trends no doubt also influence individuals' perceptions of their own fates and of how just or equitable the process is. We believe that understanding these trends and perceptions will be critical to the political sustainability of market policies across a wide range of countries.

4

Happiness, Markets, and Democracy: Latin America, Russia, and the United States

"The grumbling rich man may well be less happy than a contented peasant, but he does have a higher standard of living than the peasant."

AMARTYA SEN (1983)

A fundamental objective of public policy is to enhance the welfare of as many people as possible within a given set of resource constraints. Yet academic and public policy debates rarely address the question of what determines improvements in welfare or life satisfaction. Most economic models assume that wealth and utility are virtually synonymous. Yet research by both economists and psychologists on life satisfaction, or happiness, finds a seeming paradox that challenges that assumption: aggregate levels of life satisfaction do not increase as societies grow wealthier, even though within countries wealthier individuals are, for the most part, "happier" than poorer ones.[1] These findings highlight one of the framing themes

---

1. The economics research on happiness was pioneered by Richard Easterlin in the mid-1970s. See Easterlin (1974, 1995, 2000). For a recent study on the United Kingdom and the United States, see Blanchflower and Oswald (1999); for Switzerland, see Frey and Stutzer (1999). On measurement issues see Van Praag and Frijters (1999). For an excellent summary of the psychological work on the subject, see Kahneman, Diener, and Schwarz (1999). For a review of much of this literature, see Veenhoven (1991) and Graham and Pettinato (2001).

of this book: the importance of relative rather than absolute differences in wealth, particularly after societies cross a certain absolute level of income. We also argue that the persistence of such differences may be more important than their initial emergence to assessments of well-being (the tunnel effect hypothesis) and that individuals' expectations of future progress or mobility play important mediating effects in their attitudes about relative income differences (the POUM hypothesis). As we have noted throughout the book, concerns about relative income differences—which are mediated by expectations for the future—can also have political ramifications and, in particular, result in persistent attitudes about redistribution.[2]

Although not the usual subject of analysis, nonincome determinants of economic behavior and attitudes about relative income differences are likely to have some influence on the future direction of market economies in both developed and developing countries. Our focus on relative income differences and expectations for future progress by no means discounts the fundamental importance of economic growth in reducing poverty and attaining a wide range of other development objectives. It does suggest, however, that factors other than income growth affect individuals' assessments of their own welfare, as well as their responses to public policies and incentives.

The issue of relative income differences is a particularly salient one for the emerging market countries, where macroeconomic policy frameworks are in flux and there is wide debate over who the winners and losers are. In addition, the new opportunities and increased mobility that accompany the turn to the market also come with new insecurities.[3] Our survey research in Peru, discussed in detail in chapter 5, suggests that even the winners may be reluctant to assess their situation positively and, in line with the general direction of the happiness literature findings, that the relationship between wealth and happiness is not straightforward.[4] Yet little is known about how the turn to the market and related macroeconomic trends affect individual perceptions of current and future well-being or happiness or about how those aggregate at the country level.

The literature on market reforms has focused on aggregate measures of support for markets, evaluating governments' records at implementing

---

2. Benabou and Ok (1998), Clifford and Heath (1993), and Piketty (1995).
3. For a description of these insecurities and their causes, see Rodrik (1999).
4. Graham and Pettinato (2001); see also Webb (2000).

reforms and then on the public's approval or disapproval of these reforms, using electoral outcomes as a proxy.[5] No attempt has been made to evaluate the effects of reforms and related macroeconomic trends on individuals' subjective well-being or the influence of those perceptions on public support for market policies. Moreover, although much of the literature suggests a virtuous and self-reinforcing link between markets and democracy, little, if any, analysis of this link has been conducted at the individual level. In other words, is there a direct link between individuals' support for the market and their support (or lack thereof) for democratic government? We attempt to shed light on some of these issues through our analysis of new data from Latin America.[6]

In this chapter we explore three propositions related to the contextual variables introduced in the first chapter. The first is that the standard demographic determinants of happiness in advanced industrial economies also hold for Latin America. The second is that relative differences matter more than absolute ones, resulting in a marked gap between individuals' absolute income levels and their subjective evaluations of their well-being. In developing countries this gap may also be driven by volatility and insecurity, which is more prevalent in those economies than in advanced industrial ones. From the regionwide data, we find some evidence of the kinds of gaps between individuals' subjective evaluations of their past economic progress and actual trends, such as those we find in Peru, where the most upwardly mobile individuals in our panel of households are the most negative in their subjective evaluations of their past progress.[7]

The third proposition is that macroeconomic trends, such as rates of inflation and unemployment, have significant effects on subjective well-being, even after taking sociodemographic effects into account. In addition, in countries undertaking market reforms, public tolerance for relative income differences is moderated by the extent to which more immediate concerns, such as high levels of inflation or unemployment, have been resolved. As Hirschman suggests, when such concerns are paramount, the

---

5. See, among others, Geddes (1995); Graham (1994, 1998); and Haggard and Webb (1994).

6. An earlier version of this chapter was published as Graham and Pettinato (2001).

7. See Graham and Pettinato (forthcoming), where the determinants of this gap are explored in detail using Peru panel data and a panel of Russian households.

initial appearance of inequality may be a signal of positive economic change. Its persistence is what causes frustration.

An additional component of our analysis is an exploration of the effects of market reforms and related trends on individuals' life satisfaction. We focus on the effects of inflation and unemployment on life satisfaction and on attitudes about markets and democracy and then examine the links among life satisfaction, pro-market attitudes, and attitudes about democracy.

Our analysis is based on data from a regionwide opinion survey, the Latinobarometro, which was conducted annually in seventeen countries from 1997 to 2000.[8] This includes Brazil and all of the Spanish-speaking countries in the region, except Cuba and the Dominican Republic. Unless otherwise specified, the results reported here are from the final year of the sample, 2000, which has the most complete questionnaire. Where possible, we used the entire pooled sample to check the robustness of findings. The pooled sample has the advantage of being a time series; its disadvantage is that several of the most pertinent life satisfaction questions are not included in all of the years. For a subset of questions, we are able to provide comparable evidence for Russia from the Russian Longitudinal Monitoring Survey and for the United States from the General Social Survey.

Happiness in Latin America

We explored the usual sociodemographic variables that influence happiness, such as age, income, employment and marital status, and education levels, using an approach that others have used for the developed economies. Our dependent variable, happiness, is constructed from a question from the Latinobarometro survey about individuals' degree of life sat-

---

8. Approximately 1,000 interviews were conducted in each country, giving us over 17,000 observations a year upon which to base our statistical analysis. The poll is conducted by a respected private firm, MORI (the Chile-based Latin American branch of the London company), with the support of the European Commission and the Inter-American Development Bank. The effort began in 1995 with a subset of countries; full coverage began in 1997. A clear limitation is that the data are not nationally representative in all of the countries, and a sharp urban bias is present in several. One of the authors, Graham, was involved in the launch of the survey while on a fellowship at the Inter-American Development Bank (IDB). She continues to provide input on the design of the survey each year and therefore has access to the MORI data set. Because MORI still has to cover costs, the most recent data are available to the public only for purchase. Lagged data are available free of charge from the IDB.

Table 4-1. *Happiness, Sociodemographics, and Perceptions,*
Latin America, 2000[a]

| Independent variable | Happiness | | | |
| | 1 | | 2 | |
	Coefficient	z statistic	Coefficient	z statistic
Age	−0.025	−4.216	−0.014	−2.193
Age²/100	0.025	3.802	0.017	2.412
Male	0.060	1.750	0.080	2.194
Log wealth	0.463	12.066	0.285	6.722
Education	0.006	1.239	−0.007	−1.432
Married	0.090	2.594	0.082	2.210
Employment status				
Self-employed	−0.070	−1.465	−0.089	−1.731
Public employee	0.015	0.223	−0.025	−0.335
Private employee	0.047	0.863	0.005	0.082
Unemployed	−0.276	−3.853	−0.279	−3.659
Retired	−0.062	−0.802	−0.062	−0.749
Student	0.057	0.851	0.034	0.483
Perception of past mobility	. . .	. . .	0.370	14.237
Prospect of upward mobility	. . .	. . .	0.331	13.496
Economic ladder question	. . .	. . .	0.147	12.864
Pseudo-R^2	0.049		0.068	
Number of observations	14,760		13,139	

Source: Authors' calculations from Latinobarometro.
a. Ordered logit estimations with country dummies (coefficients not shown). Omitted reference category is housewives or husbands.

isfaction, with four possible answers: not at all satisfied, somewhat satisfied, satisfied, and very satisfied. We develop a standard regression model in which happiness is a function of a number of demographic variables, using ordered logits, both with country dummies and by treating the entire survey as one large regionwide sample without the dummies (results are shown in the first two columns of table 4-1).[9]

The regressions show that Latin America is not all that different from the advanced industrial economies. As expected, happiness has a quadratic

9. The OLS regressions with and without country fixed effects and the ordered logits with and without country dummies yielded very similar results. Results not in the tables can be obtained from the authors.

Figure 4-1. *Happiness by Age Level for Latin America, 2000*

Level of happiness

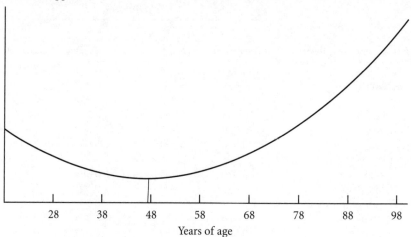

Years of age

Source: Authors' calculations based on Latinobarometro data for 2000.

relationship with age, initially decreasing, and then increasing monotonically after age 47 (figure 4-1).[10] Studies in advanced industrial economies find a similar relationship, although the low point on the happiness curve usually occurs either slightly earlier or slightly later, depending on the country.[11] As in the industrial countries, being married has positive and significant effects in Latin America. Latin America shows no significant gender effect as the advanced industrial countries do (women are slightly happier than men in the United States, for example).[12]

Also as in the industrial countries, the coefficients for level of wealth are strong, positive, and significant on happiness. When wealth is included in the regressions, the coefficient for education level is usually significant and positive but much weaker than the effects of wealth or insignificant, depending on the regressions used. With wealth and education levels highly

10. The exact age varies slightly, from 45 to 50 years of age, depending on the specifications of the regression.

11. Di Tella, MacCulloch, and Oswald (1997).

12. Although gender was not in our subset of questions from the GSS and therefore does not appear in our regressions table, other studies of happiness find that women are, on average, happier than men in the United States. See Blanchflower and Oswald (1999).

correlated, wealth effects consistently dominate in the happiness equations. When wealth is excluded, education levels have positive and significant effects on happiness. Not surprisingly, when we add a variable based on individuals' responses to their satisfaction with their financial situation, higher levels of such satisfaction have positive and significant effects on happiness, in addition to the effects of other variables including wealth.[13]

Being self-employed or unemployed has significant and negative effects on happiness in the Latin American sample. When country dummies are included, the coefficient on self-employment becomes insignificant. In advanced industrial economies, being unemployed also has negative effects on happiness, but being self-employed has positive effects. The most plausible explanation is quite intuitive: most self-employed people in advanced economies are self-employed by choice, while in developing economies, many people are self-employed, living a precarious existence in the informal sector, because of the lack of more secure employment opportunities.[14]

The Perceptions Gap

At our request, the Latinobarometro survey included several questions designed to capture any perceptions gap between where people place themselves on the income ladder and where they actually are, and the extent to which that gap is negatively skewed. In our Peru survey, upwardly mobile respondents said that they were doing worse than they actually were, and the gap was greater for those in the middle stratum than for the poorest.

We constructed variables based on three questions designed to gauge the gap between objective economic situations and subjective evaluations. The first of these was how individuals evaluate their current economic situation compared with their past situation: perceptions of past mobility (PPM).[15]

13. Indeed, when we compared the impact of the different variables using beta coefficients, the variable for satisfaction with one's personal financial situation had a much stronger effect than did individuals' level of wealth.

14. Satisfaction with democracy, which we discuss later, is also on average lower among the self-employed in Latin America. For details on the determinants of job satisfaction in the advanced industrial economies, see Clark and Oswald (1996). For detail on the determinants in Peru, see Graham and Pettinato (2001).

15. In our Peru study, we had panel data and thus precise economic information at the individual level over time to compare with the subjective assessments; see Graham and Pettinato (2000, 2001). For Latinobarometro we have cross-section information about where people are situated in one of five socioeconomic categories, an assessment that is made by the interviewer. We have also constructed a wealth index, based on a series of questions in the survey about

The second variable, the prospects of upward mobility (POUM), was based on what individuals thought their economic situation would be in a year compared with the present. The economic ladder question (ELQ) asked respondents to place themselves on a ten-step ladder representing their society, where the poor were on the first step and the rich were on the tenth. An additional question asked respondents to rank their parents, when they were their age, on the income ladder of their time.

Not surprisingly, many of the same variables that are correlated with happiness are also correlated with PPM and POUM, as is happiness itself.[16] Being wealthy increases the likelihood of individuals having a high PPM ranking, while being unemployed decreases it. Wealth also increases the likelihood of having positive prospects of upward mobility. Rather surprisingly, employment status has no significant effects: unemployed respondents are as likely to have a positive POUM as are employed ones. The POUM captures hope and expectations as well as realistic socioeconomic assessments; presumably even most unemployed people expect that their future prospects will be better than they are at present.

Responses to the ELQ revealed some evidence of a perceptions gap. The mean wealth levels of those who placed themselves on the lowest rung of the ladder were actually higher than those of respondents who placed themselves on the second rung. Mean wealth levels of those that placed themselves on the top two rungs of the ladder were lower than mean wealth levels of those respondents that placed themselves on rungs six, seven, and eight (figure 4-2).

Our analysis of a similar economic ladder question in Peru and Russia, discussed in detail in chapter 5, finds similar gaps: those who place themselves on the bottom of the ladder in those countries are, on average, underestimating their actual relative wealth, and those who place themselves on the top of the ladder overestimate their wealth.[17] Where respondents are on

---

household ownership of consumer goods ranging from indoor plumbing to cars and refrigerators. This was calculated as a simple average of the individual household possession/characteristics. A wealth index based on a Principal Components Analysis yielded virtually identical results (the correlation among the two was 99 percent). Details on the wealth index are in Graham and Pettinato (2000).

16. Regression results are available from the authors upon request.

17. Some of this result may be driven by standard bias; that is, those respondents who give extreme responses are also more likely to be incorrect in their assessments.

Figure 4-2. *Rank on Economic Ladder: Perception versus Reality*[a]

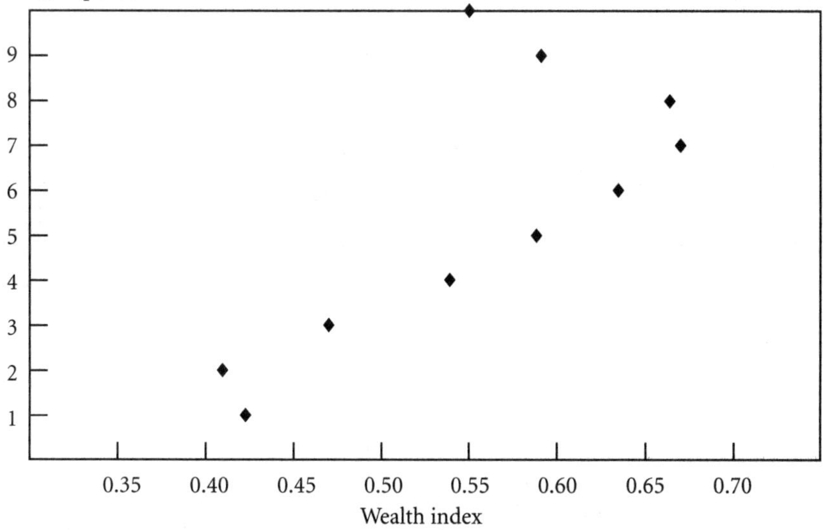

ELQ response

Source: Authors' calculations based on Latinobarometro data for 2000.

a. The figure shows the mean wealth level of respondents who placed themselves on each step of the notional economic ladder.

the income ladder and who their reference group is seem to influence how they evaluate their economic situation.[18]

These subjective evaluations, meanwhile, have effects on happiness. Positive rankings on all three of the subjective well-being variables had positive and significant effects on reported life satisfaction (second two columns of table 4-1).[19] Ranking oneself higher on the income ladder than one ranked his or her parents also had positive and significant effects on happiness. One caveat is that the direction of causality is not clear, as happier people are also more likely to have positive rankings on all three of these variables.

18. As in Hirschman's tunnel effect, people's evaluations of their own progress seem to be greatly influenced by how much those around them are progressing, and frustration arises when everyone else seems to be moving faster.

19. Using an OLS regression with standardized beta coefficients, we found that the ELQ variable has stronger effects than the PPM variable.

Regardless of causality, such perceptions gaps, in addition to being of academic interest, may also have implications for individuals' future economic behavior. A number of psychological studies in Australia and the United States, for example, find positive effects of happiness on future incomes.[20] And, at least in theory, perceptions of relative income differences can lead to "nonrational" or nonoptimal behavior, such as conspicuous consumption rather than investing in children's education. In practice, we have only anecdotal evidence of this kind of behavior in the region.[21]

Macroeconomic Trends, Pro-Market Attitudes, and Happiness

Because of the strong influence of demographic and microeconomic variables, the link between macroeconomic policies and individuals' life satisfaction or happiness is complex. Still, Di Tella and colleagues find that, above and beyond the effects of the usual sociodemographic variables such as age, gender, and employment status, inflation and unemployment have negative effects on happiness in both the United Kingdom and the United States.[22] It is quite plausible that macroeconomic trends have significant effects on individuals' life satisfaction in the emerging market countries, where far-reaching changes in the policy framework and in macroeconomic outcomes, such as the stabilization of high levels of inflation, are part and parcel of the reform process.

Evaluating the effects of market reforms in general on life satisfaction is more difficult than capturing the isolated effects of inflation or unemployment, in large part because of difficulties in evaluating individual countries' progress on reform. Reform indexes compiled at particular points in time are useful tools for gauging the extent to which the policy framework has changed during a fixed period of time.[23] They are far less effective, however,

20. In the United States these effects are moderated by parents' incomes; that is, the effects are stronger for individuals from economically advantaged backgrounds. See Diener and Biswas-Diener (1999); see also Argyle (1999), and Kenny (1999).

21. Several isolated studies have found that high school students—often the best students—are dropping out of school because they do not have the resources necessary to attend university and cannot break out of their parents' occupational category with only a high school degree. At the same time, they are readily able to find employment and purchase consumer goods without a secondary school degree. Authors' interview with Marta Lagos, who carried out an education survey for UNICEF in Chile. For Brazil, see Perlman (1999).

22. Di Tella, MacCulloch, and Oswald (1997).

23. See for example, Lora and Londoño (1998); Morley, Machado, and Pettinato (1999).

in gauging the effectiveness of the policies implemented. They also have a time-lag problem. Chile, for example, which has gone further than most countries in the region in implementing reforms, usually scores quite low on these indexes, because it implemented most of its reforms before 1985 and the typical period used for evaluating the reform record in the region is 1985–95.

This time lag issue is particularly pertinent to analysis of public opinion. Several studies find that publics tend to favor reform more strongly in its early stages, when the collective memory of economic crisis and high infla-tion in particular is still vivid.[24] As reforms are consolidated and memory fades, publics are likely to pay more attention to distribution issues. In ear-lier work, based on a question in the 1998 Latinobarometro, we found that in poor countries mostly in the early stages of reform, respondents are more likely to favor productivity over redistribution as the key to their country's moving forward. In wealthier countries, where reforms are more consoli-dated (and social welfare institutions more developed), respondents are more likely to favor redistribution. Overall, 44 percent of respondents in the sample favored redistribution, while a majority, 53 percent, favored pro-ductivity (figure 4-3).[25]

Across the board, pro-market views are stronger in Latin American countries that are in the early stages of reform. Generally, market reforms produce increased inequality in the short term. But they also create new opportunities for mobility and advancement. In addition, tangible benefits from reforms in the early stages, such as the reduction of inflation, con-tribute to favorable public opinion. And the reforms often take place during the new leaders' political honeymoons, which are enhanced by the demon-stration of political will necessary to implement difficult reforms.

In our analysis, the latecomers to reform—countries that were imple-menting reforms at a rapid pace but were still in the early phases when the surveys were conducted—have higher POUM levels than the "slow pio-neers" now in their second stage of reforms (figure 4-4). These later-stage reforms are often more difficult to implement, as they challenge entrenched interest groups in public sector institutions, and have a much longer lag in

---

24. See, for example, Graham (1999); Graham and Pettinato (2000); Stokes (1996).
25. This stands in sharp contrast to Russia, where 75 percent of surveyed respondents favor restricting the incomes of the rich.

Figure 4-3. *Productivity versus Redistribution, Latin America, 1998*[a]

Percent productivity supporters

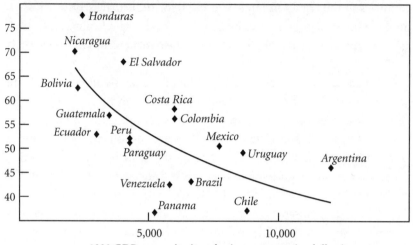

1998 GDP per capita (purchasing power parity dollars)

Source: Authors' calculations based on Latinobarometro data for 1999 and World Bank data for GDP per capita.

a. The figure shows mean country-level scores on a question asking whether respondents thought their country needed more productivity or more redistribution to get ahead. $R^2 = 0.51$.

delivering results.[26] A high pro-market score in a country like Venezuela, which has not progressed as far in reforms as has Chile, where the process is nearly complete but which has a lower score, may also reflect differences in the absolute levels of progress and in the marginal benefits from further reforms as much as genuine differences in public opinion about the market across countries.

Our hypothesis about the effects of the timing and maturity of reforms is supported by the mixed relationship between POUM rankings and support for productivity (versus redistribution). Indeed, Chile, one of the countries with the most extensive reform trajectory but an average POUM ranking, had the lowest percentage of respondents in the region in favor of productivity.

26. For second-stage reforms, see Graham and Naím (1998). See also Pastor and Wise (1999).

Figure 4-4. *Structural Reform and the Prospect of Upward Mobility, Latin America, 1998*[a]

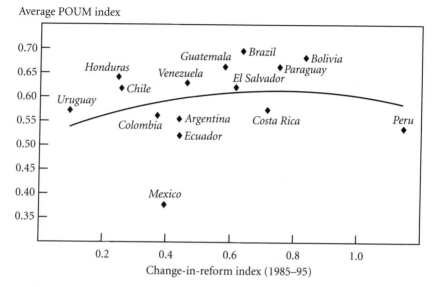

Average POUM index

Change-in-reform index (1985–95)

Source: Authors' calculations based on Latinobarometro data for 1999 and Morley, Machado, and Pettinato (1999) for reform indexes.

a. The figure shows mean country-level scores on the POUM index compared with country's ranking on an index that measures the extent of progress in implementing reforms from 1985 to 1995.

A related issue in explaining support for redistribution is the state's capacity to respond to the perceived need for redistribution with effective policies. In the United States in the 1930s, economic instability and the prospects of downward mobility for the middle class resulted in an alliance between the middle class and the poor in support of redistributive policies, which were institutionalized in the New Deal.[27] In Latin America, the increased insecurity in labor markets and the decline of social insurance of the 1980s and 1990s has instead been accompanied by heightened prospects for upward mobility, at least for skilled workers, and a generalized erosion of confidence in the state's ability to redistribute fairly and efficiently.

27. Rodrik (1999).

Cultural and institutional differences can also play a role in determining people's attitudes toward redistribution. In this case, however, the two countries with the strongest tradition of good social welfare services in the region, Chile and Costa Rica, have completely different outcomes: Chile had the lowest percentage of productivity supporters, whereas Costa Rica had one of the highest. Costa Rica, in contrast to Chile, has made much less progress implementing structural reforms such as privatization, a fact that supports our hypothesis on the timing of reforms.

These findings also support our initial emphasis on relative versus absolute income levels: in poorer Latin American countries such as Bolivia and those in Central America, people accord issues of absolute income— growth, for example—more importance than those of distribution, even when inequality levels are high.[28] In wealthier countries such as Argentina, Chile, and Venezuela, issues of inequality and distribution may be accorded more importance in the public debate.[29] Note, however, that concern about inequality as expressed in public debate does not necessarily translate into votes for higher taxes, particularly in countries with high POUM levels.

Combined, these factors may explain our statistical findings. The effects of both our reform index (status of reforms in 1995) and our change-in-reform index (an index we developed that explains how extensive the reform implementation efforts were in a particular country during the 1985–95 period) were both negative and significant on happiness. Yet if one looks at average happiness levels by country (which does not account for differences in attitudes among individuals within countries), the results demonstrate no distinguishable relationship between happiness and reform progress.[30] As is shown in figure 4-5, some of the strongest reformers, such

28. The links that Sen (1983) draws between absolute and relative income and the dependence of these links on one's relative position are worth noting here. Not owning leather shoes, for example, is hardly deprivation in an absolute sense. But in many societies, it could make one ineligible for a number of jobs.

29. See Graham and Pettinato (2000) for correlation tables. This was further supported by a simple cross-country empirical exercise for the region in which we regressed the pro-market index on the level of reform in 1985, controlling for the change in reform in 1985–95, growth, and gross domestic product per capita in 1997. The results supported the negative impact of the level of reform in 1985 on the average pro-reform index. With the exception of Peru, the POUM scores for the fast and late reformers also tended to be higher compared with those of the slow and early reformers.

30. Because of the mixed and largely insignificant nature of these results, we do not report them here. Interested readers may contact the authors directly.

Figure 4-5. *Average Happiness Levels in Latin America, 2000*

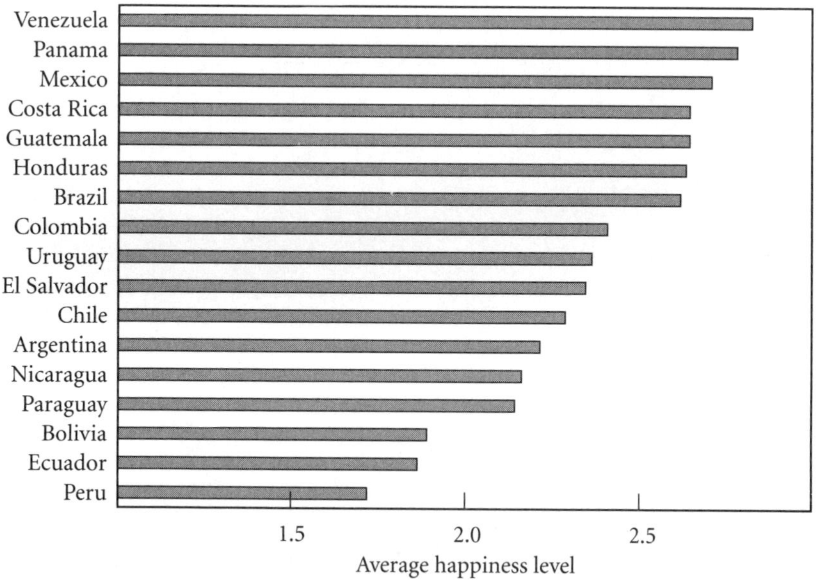

Average happiness level

Source: Authors' calculations based on Latinobarometro data for 2000.

as Peru, have very low average happiness levels, and others, like Mexico, have high average levels. Moreover, some of those countries with the worst reform records in the region, such as Venezuela, have the highest happiness levels, while others with poor records, such as Ecuador, have very low happiness levels. Happiness levels in some of the most successful reformers, such as Chile and Uruguay, were moderate to high.

In contrast to aggregate country-level indexes of reform, individual respondents' attitudes about the market were positively correlated with happiness.[31] In other words, controlling for other variables such as income and age and using country dummies, individuals with pro-market attitudes were, on average, happier than those who did not favor market policies. Not surprisingly, wealth levels and education levels had positive and significant effects on pro-market attitudes (table 4-2).

31. The pro-market index was constructed on the basis of how individuals answered three questions about their support for privatization, price liberalization, and the market economy. Each question had four possible answers, which were equally weighted and normalized on a 0 to 1 scale to construct the index.

Table 4-2. *Correlates of Pro-Market Attitudes, Latin America, 2000*[a]

Independent variable	Pro-market attitudes index			
	Coefficient	t statistic	Coefficient	t statistic
Age	−0.003	−3.46	−0.003	−3.18
Age²/100	0.003	3.19	0.003	2.93
Male	0.017	3.25	0.016	3.15
Log wealth	0.057	9.66	0.052	8.87
Education	0.001	2.18	0.001	2.08
Married	−0.004	−0.70	−0.005	−0.88
Employment status				
Self-employed	0.001	0.07	0.001	0.18
Public employee	−0.009	−0.87	−0.008	−0.80
Private employee	0.000	0.05	0.000	0.04
Unemployed	−0.021	−1.91	−0.017	−1.52
Retired	−0.002	−0.13	−0.001	−0.04
Student	0.030	−3.02	−0.031	−3.09
Happy	. . .	. . .	0.022	9.50
Intercept	0.578	27.3	0.517	23.41
R^2	0.014		0.021	
Number of observations	11,928		11,854	

Source: Authors' calculations from Latinobarometro.
a. Country fixed-effects estimation. Omitted reference category is housewives or husbands.

When we look at the inverse relationship, we also find that happier people are more likely to be pro-market, so we have the usual problem of establishing the direction of causality. It may well be that happier individuals are more likely to cast whatever policy environment they inhabit in a favorable light. A brief look at the effects of macroeconomic trends on pro-market attitudes, however, suggests that there is some variance in attitudes that is not explained by personal attributes or character traits.

Controlling for the usual demographic variables such as age, income, and education, we find that the inflation rate has positive and significant effects on pro-market attitudes, while the effects of the unemployment rate are insignificant. Thus people who live in countries with high inflation rates (at the time of the survey, Ecuador and Venezuela had double-digit inflation rates) are more likely to express favorable attitudes toward the market.[32] This finding supports our timing-of-reform hypothesis: people are more

32. Venezuela has the highest mean pro-market responses in the region, and Ecuador is among the highest.

likely to favor reforms when the costs of not reforming are immediately obvious or still fresh in the collective memory.[33]

Interestingly enough, although the unemployment rate was insignificant, *concerns* about unemployment (which were captured in a separate question about how much respondents feared losing their job in the future) had positive and significant effects on pro-market attitudes. The actual rate of unemployment may have weak effects because formal unemployment rates are quite low for most Latin American countries. In the absence of unemployment insurance, very few people can "afford" to be unemployed but are instead underemployed or in the informal sector. Thus the effects of concerns about unemployment are stronger than the actual rates.[34] Concern for inflation, meanwhile, was insignificant. It is likely that the effects of real inflation rates outweigh the effects of concern for inflation in the few countries where inflation is high.[35]

As in the case of pro-market attitudes, concern for inflation and joblessness had different effects on happiness than the actual rates of inflation and unemployment. Although being unemployed has significant and negative effects on happiness, expressing concern about unemployment has no significant effects on happiness, nor does the rate of unemployment. The actual rate of inflation has significant and negative effects on happiness, similar to those Di Tella and colleagues find for the United States and the United Kingdom (second two columns in table 4-3). This effect contrasts with the positive effects that inflation has on pro-market attitudes. These findings make intuitive sense: high inflation has substantial costs for most people's standard of living and is therefore likely to make individuals favor market policies as a way to reduce inflation. At the same time, as long as the inflation continues, it is likely to reduce people's subjective well-being. *Concerns* about inflation have no significant effects.

33. Using prospect theory to evaluate voters' tolerance for difficult reform measures, Weyland (1998) finds that they are much more likely to support such measures when future prospects seem better than the current conditions and that they become much more conservative once better conditions are established.

34. A possible econometric explanation for this problem—known as the Moulton bias—stems from including one or more aggregate variables in a regression based on individual-level variables.

35. To avoid too many detailed tables, we report only the results on the rates and not on concerns here. The regression equations that include all of these variables appear in Graham and Pettinato (2001) and are also available from the authors on request.

Market Attitudes and Democracy

One of the most difficult questions facing social scientists in an age of dual transitions to democracy and the market is the relationship between these two trends. A wide body of literature has explored these relationships, with some proponents arguing that progress in one of the two areas must logically precede the other, while others argue that the two trends are self-reinforcing.[36] We by no means attempt to take on these difficult questions here. Our findings, however, may provide some insights for the debate.

Our Latinobarometro sample had two questions pertaining to democracy. One asked respondents whether democracy was preferable to any other form of government. The other inquired about the respondent's degree of satisfaction with democracy, with four possible answers: not at all satisfied, not very satisfied, satisfied, and very satisfied. When we examined the effects of these two variables on happiness, controlling for the usual sociodemographic variables and including country dummies, we found that satisfaction with democracy was correlated with higher levels of happiness, while a preference for democracy over other forms of government had no significance. When we included pro-market attitudes in the regression, the effects of satisfaction with democracy remained positive and significant (table 4-3). The combined positive effects of pro-market attitudes and satisfaction with democracy on life satisfaction give us some cause for guarded optimism about a reinforcing virtuous circle.

These findings are in keeping with those of Ronald Inglehart, who uses data on life satisfaction and political satisfaction from the Eurobarometer survey for nine European nations from 1973 to 1986 (totaling more than 200,000 interviews in more than 200 nationally representative surveys). Inglehart finds that at the aggregate country level both political satisfaction and life satisfaction are correlated with stable democracy. The effects of life satisfaction are stronger, however, because life satisfaction trends within developed countries are fairly stable over time and seem to be correlated with other traits such as interpersonal trust. In contrast, political satisfaction fluctuates more, because it behaves like an indicator of public attitudes

---

36. For a number of different views and approaches on this topic, see Carothers (1999); Graham, (1998); Haggard and Kaufman (1995); Haggard and Webb (1994), and Przeworski (1991).

Table 4-3. *Happiness, Market, and Democracy Preferences,*
Latin America, 2000

	Happiness			
	1		2	
Independent variable	Coefficient	z statistic	Coefficient	z statistic
Age	−0.014	−1.99	−0.008	−1.24
Age²/100	0.011	1.46	0.001	0.13
Male	0.050	1.29	0.036	0.92
Log wealth	0.361	8.08	0.632	15.11
Education	0.005	1.01	−0.031	−6.34
Married	0.091	2.30	0.054	1.35
Employment status				
Self-employed	−0.083	−1.50	−0.110	−1.98
Public employee	−0.041	−0.53	0.035	0.45
Private employee	0.000	0.00	0.026	0.42
Unemployed	−0.310	−3.81	−0.294	−3.63
Retired	−0.082	−0.88	−0.030	−0.33
Student	0.091	1.22	0.049	0.66
Pro-democracy dummy	−0.017	−0.48	−0.132	−3.63
Satisfaction with democracy	0.307	14.68	0.362	18.28
Pro-market attitudes	0.543	7.85	0.521	7.70
Inflation rate			−0.007	−4.96
Unemployment rate			−0.004	−0.75
Pseudo-R^2	0.058		0.027	
Number of observations	14,255		11,197	

Source: Authors' calculations from Latinobarometro.

a. Ordered logit estimations with country dummies in (1) (country coefficients not shown) and without country dummies in (2). Omitted reference categories are not married; and house-wives or husbands.

about government popularity, changing from one month to the next in response to current economic and political events. Political satisfaction levels are only weakly linked ($r = 0.21$ for the whole sample) with the number of years that democratic institutions have been in place in a given nation (Inglehart's measure of stable democracy), while the link between life satisfaction and stable democracy is higher ($r = 0.85$).[37]

Looking more closely at the *determinants* of attitudes about and satisfaction with democracy, we find that wealth and education levels have no

37. Inglehart (1988).

Table 4-4. *Democracy: Preferences and Satisfaction, Latin America, 2000*[a]

Independent variable	Pro-democracy dummy		Satisfaction with democracy	
	Coefficient	z statistic	Coefficient	z statistic
Age	0.018	2.606	−0.018	−2.881
Age^2/100	−0.011	−1.374	0.025	3.561
Male	0.135	3.409	−0.026	−0.748
Log wealth	0.184	4.303	0.054	1.363
Education	0.043	8.480	0.003	0.638
Married	0.068	1.695	0.015	0.415
Employment status				
Self-employed	−0.018	−0.335	−0.140	−2.827
Public employee	0.120	1.493	0.124	1.758
Private employee	0.103	1.633	−0.057	−1.021
Unemployed	0.081	1.003	−0.133	−1.795
Retired	0.094	1.030	−0.119	−1.484
Student	0.356	4.612	−0.085	−1.236
Pseudo-R^2	0.063		0.065	
Number of observations	14,879		14,357	

Source: Authors' calculations from Latinobarometro.

a. Respectively, logit and ordered logit estimations with country dummies (coefficients not shown). Omitted reference category is housewives or husbands.

significant correlation with satisfaction with democracy but that they do have a positive and significant correlation with a preference for democracy over other systems (table 4-4). This is not surprising, in part because of the correlation between life satisfaction and political satisfaction, and in part because of the expected effects of education on political attitudes. Being self-employed has insignificant effects on preference for democracy, but it has negative and significant effects on satisfaction with democracy. One can imagine that a precariously employed individual in the informal sector might prefer democracy as a system, but not be particularly satisfied with how the government (or the economy) is performing.

A Comparative Look: Some Evidence from Russia

For some, but by no means all, of the questions above, we were able to obtain comparable data for Russia and the United States. The RLMS, which provides panel data for approximately 2,000 households in Russia for 1995

Table 4-5. *Happiness in Russia, 1998–99*[a]

Independent variable	Happiness			
	1		*2*	
	Coefficient	z statistic	Coefficient	z statistic
Age	−0.141	−3.685	−0.052	−2.697
Age²/100	0.155	3.684	0.054	3.04
Gender (male = 1)	0.396	3.079	0.438	4.365
Log income	0.455	7.261	...	...
Change in log income	...	...	1.054	3.299
Years of education	−0.025	−0.522	0.054	2.36
Marital (married = 1)	0.03	0.251	0.1	1.063
Employment status				
Self-employed	0.43	1.025	0.525	1.228
Employee	−0.066	−0.264	−0.137	−0.722
Unemployed	0.965	1.317	−0.737	−2.956
Retired	−0.725	−0.462	−0.63	−2.898
Student	...	...	−0.209	−0.246
Fear of job loss	−0.232	−5.672	...	...
Pseudo-R^2	0.049		0.017	
Number of observations	1,195		2,003	

Source: Authors' calculations from Russia Longitudinal Monitoring Survey (various issues).

a. Ordered logit estimation. Calculated as the percentage change in log-adjusted household income between 1995 and 1999; see text box 3-1 for explanation.

through 1998, included a life satisfaction question as well as other questions comparable to some of those in the Latinobarometro.[38]

The determinants of happiness in Russia are very similar to those for Latin America, according to these data (table 4-5). Not surprisingly, income has positive and significant effects on happiness, which seem to outweigh the effects of education level, as was the case in Latin America. Rather surprisingly, and in contrast to Latin America and the advanced industrial countries, being married did not have any significant effects on happiness in Russia. Men, meanwhile, were happier than women in Russia, in contrast to Latin America, where there was no consistent gender effect. Fear of losing one's job had significant and negative effects. Unemployment had significant and negative effects when fear of losing one's job was not in the

38. More information and access to data on the RLMS can be found at (www.cpc.unc.edu/projects/rlms/).

equation, but when the latter was included, the unemployment variable was rendered insignificant.[39]

We also looked at the effects of the variation in incomes (income mobility, using 1992 rubles) between 1995 and 1998 on happiness. In general, income variations had no significant effects on happiness, but when we used the percentage change in log income rather than in absolute levels of income in the regressions, we found strongly positive and significant effects (see table 4-5). This logarithmic effect suggests that the same percentage change in income has larger effects on subjective well-being for those at the bottom of the income ladder than for those higher up. In other words, absolute income changes matter more for the poor, whereas after a certain absolute standard is met, relative income differences matter more.

As we discuss in chapter 5, these findings run in the same direction as those from our Peru survey, in which individuals higher up the income ladder are less satisfied with their income gains than are those lower down the ladder whose gains were smaller. Indeed, when we compare Peruvian and Russian respondents' assessments of their past progress, we find that a very similar and surprisingly high percentage of upwardly mobile individuals in both samples assess their progress as "negative" or "very negative" (44 percent in Peru and 71 percent in Russia).[40]

We looked at the effects of perceptions of past progress, expectations for the future, and notional societal status on happiness in Russia. As in Latin America, evaluating one's present situation in a positive light compared to the past, having positive prospects for the future, and placing oneself higher on the economic ladder all had positive and significant effects on happiness.[41] These perceptions, in turn, seem to affect attitudes about redistribution.

Ravallion and Loshkin examine responses to a question on the 1996 RLMS survey about whether the respondent favors restricting the incomes of the rich, a question designed to gauge public attitudes about redistribution.

---

39. The percent of the sample formally registered as unemployed was less than 1 percent.

40. These findings are discussed in much greater detail in Graham and Pettinato (forthcoming).

41. Using a standard OLS regression and normalizing the variables with beta weights, the beta weights of all three subjective indicators: PPM, POUM, and ELQ, were higher than that of log income or fear of unemployment. The ELQ for Russia had nine steps, instead of the ten found in the Latin American ELQ.

They find less support for redistribution among respondents who have positive assessments of their subjective well-being, and, inversely, more support for redistribution among those who fear that their income will fall in the future.[42] They also find that support for redistribution is higher in families where the number of pensioners is higher and among women, those living in rural areas, those who had voted for Communist party candidates in the last election, and those who feared losing their jobs. Our own research on the RLMS for 1995–98 finds similar patterns of support for redistribution.

Another trend may affect public attitudes about redistribution and individual economic status in Russia. According to Milanovic and Jovanovic, expectations are falling, and the subjective poverty line, that is, the amount of income people believe they need to make ends meet, has declined since 1995. Thus it is more "normal" to consider oneself poor or near poor. Another feature of the Russian situation is that those in the poorest income decile live primarily in what Gaddy and Ickes have termed the virtual economy: the large sector of the Russian population that lives outside the monetary economy, growing their own food and receiving wages in kind rather than in cash.[43]

As in Latin America, having a pro-market attitude has positive and significant effects on happiness in Russia, suggesting that people in both regions who favor the ongoing turn to the market are in general more satisfied. Not surprisingly, having a pro-market attitude had significant and negative effects on the likelihood of respondents supporting redistribution, as did having positive prospects for the future (a high POUM). Age, meanwhile, had a positive and significant effect on restricting the incomes of the rich, with no quadratic relationship, suggesting that support for such a restriction increases monotonically with age in Russia.[44]

Information about democratic attitudes in Russia was not comparable to that supplied by the Latinobarometro.[45] One question in the RLMS asks respondents whether they want to return to pre-Gorbachev (pre-perestroika) times. Although a very crude indicator at best, this question was included in some of our regressions as a proxy indicator of respondents'

42. Ravallion and Loshkin (1999b). The 1996 survey they used provided 7,000 responses.
43. See Milanovic and Jovanovic (1999); Gaddy and Ickes (1998).
44. For details on regressions not reported in the tables, please contact the authors directly.
45. There is, of course, more detailed work on democratic attitudes in Russia, based on other survey data. See, for example, Evans and Whitefield (1996); Rose and McAllister (1996).

preference for democracy over communism. We found that not wanting to return to communism, like having a pro-market attitude, had positive and significant effects on happiness. Again, the direction of causality is not clear, and it may well be that happy people are supportive of whatever policy environment they live in.

Still, there is some evidence of a virtuous pro-democracy, pro-market, happiness circle in Russia, as in Latin America. In Russia, however, that circle appears to be much smaller: 45 percent of respondents want to return to pre-*perestroika* days, while 75 percent of all respondents favor restricting the incomes of the rich. Ravallion and Loshkin find that redistribution in Russia is opposed not only by the rich, but also by the upwardly mobile poor. Even so, because downward income mobility is so much more prevalent, 72 percent of all respondents in Russia support redistribution.[46] In Latin America, only 44 percent of respondents favor redistribution over productivity, and 63 percent of all respondents think democracy is preferable to any other political system. The significant upward, as well as downward, mobility in Latin America explains some of the differences in attitudes about redistribution between the region and Russia.

A Comparative Look at an Advanced Economy: Evidence from the United States

In an incomplete effort that still provides a useful comparative reference from an advanced industrial economy, we looked at some similar questions for the United States. The cumulative database available from the General Social Survey (GSS) covers 30,000 individuals for the years 1972 through 1993 and includes questions about life satisfaction and individuals' satisfaction with their current income situation.[47] Like Latinobarometro, the GSS is not a panel.

As in most other countries, happiness in the United States shows a quadratic relationship with age, with the bottom of the curve being at age 43, and happiness increasing monotonically thereafter.[48] We find, not surpris-

---

46. Ravallion and Loshkin (1999b).

47. This is the same data set that Di Tella, MacCulloch, and Oswald (1997) use to analyze happiness in the United States.

48. We include year fixed effects because the combined sample is a time series.

Table 4-6. *Happiness in the United States, 1970s–1990s*[a]

Independent variable	Happiness	
	Coefficient	z statistic
Age	−0.020	−4.86
Age^2	0.023	5.27
Income in constant 1998 dollars	0.000	2.07
Education level	0.035	8.55
Male	−0.161	−6.90
Married	0.836	32.48
Employment status		
Unemployed	−0.433	−6.30
Retired	0.096	2.07
Student	0.288	4.04
Perceived past mobility	0.284	16.86
Economic satisfaction	0.616	33.97
Pseudo R^2	0.0763	
Number of observations	31,611	

Source: Authors' calculations from the General Social Survey.
a. Ordered logit estimations with year fixed effects (not shown).

ingly, positive and significant effects of both income and education on happiness, with the effects and direction of the other variables remaining constant. Being married has positive and significant effects on happiness, as does having more years of education. Women are significantly happier than men in the United States. And, as in all the other countries for which we have data, being unemployed has significant and negative effects on happiness. Being satisfied with one's personal economic situation has strong and positive effects. Adding a variable that accounts for the perception of changes in one's economic situation also produces significant and positive effects on happiness (table 4-6).

We also looked at the determinants of satisfaction with one's personal economic situation and found a quadratic relationship with age, with age 27 as the turning point. Not surprisingly, the effects of happiness are significant and positive on economic satisfaction. Here again there is the inevitable question of causality: are happier people more likely to evaluate their situation positively, or does a positive economic situation make people happier?

The answer is probably both. As noted above, several studies find that happiness has some links to future economic success.[49]

Finally, we also tried to find evidence of a perceptions gap. Although the GSS has no economic ladder question, it does ask respondents to place themselves in one of four classes. Five percent of the sample placed themselves in the lower class, 45 percent in the working class, 45 percent in the middle class, and 3 percent in the upper class. Although a sociological analysis of the class composition of the United States is well beyond the scope of this chapter, the objective data on income trends in recent years suggest a real shrinking of those in the middle income categories and a skew toward the upper tail.[50] According to an income-based measure of the middle class—the population group with incomes between 75 percent and 125 percent of median income—only 24 percent of the U.S. population was in that category in 1999, and that group held only 17.6 percent of national income. And both population and income shares were smaller than they were at the beginning of the 1990s.[51] The skew on responses about the class or category that people place themselves in, however, seems to be toward the middle rather than toward the tails.

Although the comparison is extremely crude, this finding is an apparent contrast with both Latin America and Russia, where respondents tend to underestimate their income and position on the national income ladder or to consider themselves poor. One possible explanation for the U.S. trend is that the majority of Americans still see the United States as the land of opportunity—a country where individual effort is more important than family background in determining outcomes—and that this belief holds even for those well below the mean income. Indeed, more than 150 years ago, de Tocqueville suggested that the prevalence of this belief was one of the important underpinnings of American democracy.[52]

More recently, Benabou and Ok posit that the continued prevalence of this belief is the explanation for Americans' reluctance to vote for redistri-

---

49. Diener and Biswas-Diener (1999).

50. See, for example, Burtless (1999); Krugman (1992); McMurrer and Sawhill (1998); and Solon (1992).

51. The population share in the middle class fell by 9.2 percent from 1992, while the income share fell by 11.6 percent. For more detailed discussions of the measure and concept of the middle class, see Birdsall, Graham, and Pettinato (2000).

52. De Tocqueville (1969).

bution (even as empirical data show that this belief has less and less basis in reality).[53] Supporting their analysis with data from the Panel Survey of Income Dynamics, Benabou and Ok show theoretically how even when a large majority is below the mean income, people will not vote for redistribution if they believe they will rise above the mean income in the future. Piketty shows how past mobility experiences can have a persistent influence on attitudes toward redistribution at given current incomes.[54]

Lindert, meanwhile, finds that differences among industrial countries' political tendencies to spend on social transfers are largely explained by income skewness: the size of the gap between the rich and the middle versus that between the middle and the poor. A wider lower gap means that the middle class has less affinity with the poor and that social spending is therefore less than it would be were the gap not as wide. The United States, which has a large gap between the middle and the poor, has the lowest level of social spending of the countries in the sample.[55]

In Latin America, neither the myth nor the reality of social mobility is as prevalent as it is in the United States, and macroeconomic volatility is combined with inequality driven by high incomes at the top of the distribution and small differences between those in the middle and the poor. Thus, a plausible political economy supposition is that support for redistribution should be very high.[56] Yet reported support for increasing redistribution in Latin America is lower than for increasing productivity (44 percent compared with 53 percent); support for redistribution is higher in wealthier than in poorer countries; and there is no systematic electoral trend in the region in favor of increased redistribution.[57] In Russia, in contrast, where

53. Benabou and Ok (1998).
54. Piketty (1995). See also Clifford and Heath (1993).
55. Lindert (1996).
56. For what little evidence there is on income mobility in Latin America, see Behrman, Birdsall, and Székely (1999); and Birdsall, Graham, and Pettinato (2000). See also Dahan and Gaviria (1999). This nascent literature suggests that reforms may enhance mobility and reduce the strong effects of family background on children's occupational and education outcomes, in particular by improving financial markets and schools. And while some evidence suggests that there is a great deal of movement up and down the income ladder, it is not yet clear how much of it is permanent improvements in income and how much of it is "churning," that is, short-term movements. For an account of the persistence of family background on educational outcomes, see ECLAC (2000).
57. *Within* countries in the region, the relationship is as one would predict: poorer people are more likely to favor redistribution than are richer ones. Regression results are available from the authors on request.

the skew on perceptions is similarly negative, a much higher percentage of respondents (72 percent) favor increased redistribution.[58]

These findings do not imply that there is no support for redistribution in Latin America, nor that the region could not benefit from more efficient and effective redistributive policies. The findings do suggest that the perceptions gap does not necessarily translate into support for redistribution. The ramifications of these perceptions gaps for future economic behavior are a subject for a next stage of research, which will entail collecting new data and new kinds of data, as well as enhancing tools and methods for analyzing happiness and other subjective conditions and trends.[59]

Summary of the Findings

We explored three propositions in this chapter. Recognizing the limitations of working with subjective survey data, we found consistent patterns in the effects of both demographic and macroeconomic trends on individual assessments of subjective well-being, and in turn, of those assessments on a range of other public attitudes. For the most part, these patterns support our propositions.

The first proposition was that in Latin America, the sociodemographics of happiness were similar to those of the advanced industrial countries. We found that this was indeed the case, that Latin America looks remarkably similar to the advanced industrial economies. Russia also demonstrates similar trends, although both gender and marriage had slightly different effects there than in Latin America or the United States. These findings are hardly surprising, but they do contribute to the nascent research on happiness, which, until now, has not covered developing countries in detail.

Our second proposition was that relative differences matter more than absolute ones, and that there is a marked perceptions gap between individuals' objective economic situation and their subjective evaluations of that situation. Such a gap indeed exists in Latin America, with respondents who were slightly better off than the poorest much more likely to consider them-

---

58. As discussed earlier, the questions on redistribution are not exactly the same in the two surveys.

59. In a forthcoming paper, we attempt a simple theoretical explanation of the possible effects of these gaps on future economic behavior; see Pettinato, Hammond, and Graham (forthcoming).

selves poor than were those who actually were at the bottom of the income ladder.

The effects of variations in income on happiness in Russia were logarithmic in nature, that is, they were much stronger for those with lower absolute income levels. This finding also supports the importance of relative differences. Increases in absolute income enhance life satisfaction for those at the bottom of the income ladder but not for the sample as a whole. As people move up the ladder and have more absolute income, effects seem to be driven more by how changes in their income compare with those of others in their reference group than by absolute income losses or gains.[60] Our analysis of Peru in the next chapter also supports this conclusion.

Perceptions about both past and future mobility seem to have effects on happiness: having a higher ranking on each of our perception indicators in both Latin America and Russia—perceived past mobility, prospects of upward mobility, and position on the economic ladder—were positively correlated with happiness. Several studies find positive links between happiness and future economic performance. Our own research finds that happier people are more likely to have pro-market and pro-democratic attitudes. Thus it seems plausible to posit that the strong negative skew in the perceptions of many respondents has at least some implications for the sustainability of support for market policies and, possibly, for democracy in these countries.

Our third proposition was that, in addition to the usual demographic variables, macroeconomic trends such as inflation and unemployment have significant effects on subjective well-being, and that these effects are mediated by the timing and stage of market reforms in particular countries. We found that in Latin America, as in the United States and the United Kingdom, both inflation and being unemployed had significant and negative effects on happiness. Being unemployed had negative effects in Russia as well.[61] One distinction, though is that *fear* of unemployment, which had significant and negative effects on happiness in Latin America and Russia, seems a more relevant variable than the rate of unemployment in either place. This is not surprising given that unemployment rates in these

---

60. Our findings from our panel data and perceptions survey in Peru also run in this same general direction. See Graham and Pettinato (forthcoming).

61. The RLMS did not include a question about inflation.

economies disguise the prevalence of insecure informal sector jobs and the absence of adequate unemployment insurance. Behavioral traits may also be at play here, which make determining the direction of causality difficult: optimistic people may be happy and not fear unemployment, while pessimistic people may be unhappy and fear it more.[62]

We could not find any discernible evidence of the general effects of market reforms on happiness. Among other things, evaluating countries' reform progress is extremely difficult and fraught with time inconsistency problems. We did find that having a pro-market attitude had significant and positive effects on happiness in both Latin America and Russia. Individual satisfaction with democracy had an additional and positive effect on happiness in Latin America. In Russia, not wanting to return to communism—a question that served as a very weak proxy for attitudes about democracy—had a positive and significant effect on happiness. As cautious optimists we posit that there may be a virtuous circle for some respondents, in which pro-market attitudes, satisfaction with democracy, and life satisfaction reinforce each other.

The potential of such a virtuous circle, however, will depend on whether it includes a wide majority of the population. Positive rankings on all of these indicators are strongly linked to income and wealth levels, and there is a very strong negative skew on the perceptions of past mobility of those near, but not at, the bottom of the income ladder. Several theoretical and empirical studies suggest that past mobility experiences can form political attitudes that persist despite changes in the individual's circumstances. That in turn suggests a role for public policies that enhance mobility and make progress on national income ladders more possible for those on the middle and lower rungs and that generate a more widely held belief that upward mobility is a probability rather than a remote possibility.

62. We are grateful to George Akerlof for raising this point.

5

Frustrated Achievers: Mobility Trends and Subjective Well-Being in Peru and Russia

"Mill wrote: 'men do not desire to be rich, but to be richer than other men.'"

PIGOU (1920)

The many studies of subjective well-being or happiness referred to throughout this book suggest it might be appropriate to revisit the standard assumptions about the role of rational, material, self-interest in determining economic behavior. As reported earlier, these studies find little correlation between aggregate economic growth at the national level and average levels of happiness. On average, the wealthy are happier than the poor within individual societies, but there is no evidence that happiness increases as societies grow wealthier over time or that there are differences in levels of happiness between wealthier and poorer societies (above a certain absolute minimum level of income). These findings do not discount the critical role of growth in improving objective economic conditions, such as in reducing poverty. Rather they highlight the important role that other variables, such as relative income differences, play in subjective assessments of well-being.

We focus on how income mobility, relative income differences, and expectations about future prospects for mobility affect subjective well-being. We place particular importance on two related concepts: how changes in income levels and distribution—and the persistence of those changes—affect public attitudes about inequality (the tunnel-effect hypothesis); and how those attitudes are mediated by individuals' expectations about future income mobility (the POUM hypothesis).

Research on happiness has focused on the developed economies, in large part because adequate data are more readily available. Yet some of the factors that influence individual assessments of well-being, such as income mobility, macroeconomic volatility, and occupational status, fluctuate more in the developing countries and no doubt have implications for the happiness of individuals within those countries. Our objective in this chapter is to bring some detailed empirical evidence from two emerging market economies—Peru and Russia—to bear on these issues.

We posit that individuals' perceptions of their well-being are affected not only by the already identified individual and within-country variables that influence happiness, such as marital status, employment, and inflation, but also by several variables related to international economic integration, such as exogenously driven macroeconomic volatility, the globalization of information, increasing income mobility (both upward and downward), and inequality driven by technology-led growth. And the effects of these variables may be stronger in developing economies in the process of integrating more fully into the international economy—with the consequent effects on distribution and social mobility—than they are in the advanced industrial economies. Further, unhappiness in such contexts may have implications for the political sustainability of market reforms and for social stability more generally.

As chapter 4 showed, wealthier individuals in Latin America assess their past progress and future prospects more positively than poorer ones and have more positive views about the market. Income has a positive effect on happiness for all groups in Latin America, but the effect is stronger for poor respondents than it is for wealthier ones, supporting Easterlin's point that absolute income gains matter more for those with less wealth. We also find that the effects of demographic variables—age, marital status, and education levels—on happiness are the same for Latin America as they are in the advanced industrial economies.

In this chapter we explore three propositions using panel data from Peru and Russia. The first is that relative income differences affect subjective well-being or happiness more than absolute ones do, at least above a certain absolute level of income. The second is that respondents' position on the income ladder matters a great deal, with those in the middle of the income ladder, rather than those at the bottom, most likely to be dissatisfied with their status.[1] The third is that changes in status—conceptualized here as income mobility—have significant effects on happiness, although they do not always run in the expected direction. A component of this proposition is that expectations for future upward mobility have important mediating effects on this relationship.[2]

An additional issue, explored in less detail than the first three propositions, is the relationship between social capital and mobility. We suggest that the nature of the association or organization with which the individual is affiliated is critical to whether it facilitates upward mobility. We further argue that many of the joint survival organizations of the poor provide an essential safety net but are not likely to facilitate upward mobility and may even discourage it.

It is important to note that both Peru and Russia—which are the only two countries for which we have the kinds of detailed and comparable data that we discuss here—have very low mean happiness levels compared with most other countries (see figure 2-1). Part of the reason for these low levels of happiness may be cultural and therefore difficult to measure. Part of the

1. Distributional "stress" on the middle class, related to globalization, is discussed in Birdsall, Graham, and Pettinato (2000). In a more theoretical exploration, Robson (1992) highlights the potential "stress" on the middle sectors that arises when status as well as wealth is included in the utility function.

2. Most of the studies of the effects of social mobility on happiness were conducted several decades ago and focused on social class. When social class is assessed by asking people in the United States and Europe to rate themselves, there is a correlation with happiness of about 0.25 to 0.30. These correlations are much stronger in other countries. For example, in a study done in 1965, the correlation between happiness and objective social class is 0.55 in Israel, 0.52 in Nigeria, 0.44 in the Philippines, 0.42 in India, and 0.38 in Brazil. Class seems to have more effects on happiness in countries where income inequality is high and social mobility is low. The link between happiness and high social class, meanwhile, is much stronger in more unequal societies for which there are data, such as India, and lower for more equal ones, such as Australia; see Argyle (1999). Therefore it is plausible to assume that significant changes in mobility rates in such contexts could have some effects on happiness. A more recent study by Marshall and Firth (1999), based on data for ten countries from the International Social Justice Project, finds only weak links between class experience and satisfaction with life.

explanation no doubt lies in the very volatile macroeconomic trajectory both these countries had in the 1980s and 1990s. Low average scores should not affect the within-country analysis, however, which is the focus of this chapter. That both countries have similar scores makes our comparisons easier than they would be if one had a high level of happiness and the other a low level. Any future efforts to incorporate other countries into the analysis will have to account for biases related to the low mean scores for Peru and Russia.[3]

Economic Trends in Peru and Russia: Opportunity and Vulnerability

Both Peru and Russia have been affected by the same broad trends that most emerging market economies have experienced. Market reforms and globalization have brought economic growth and created new opportunities for many individuals in these countries. At the same time, macroeconomic volatility related to greater engagement in the global economy has threatened many others with poverty, including many of those who were once securely in the middle class.[4]

In the late 1980s Peru faced hyperinflation and unprecedented deep recession, with gross domestic product falling by roughly 25 percent between 1988 and 1990. This record was largely the result of fiscal mismanagement, exacerbated by poor management of the country's large external debt burden. Poverty rose dramatically, affecting 54 percent of the population by 1990, while public social expenditure plummeted.[5]

After a dramatic stabilization and macroeconomic adjustment program was implemented in the early 1990s, annual growth reached 14 percent in

3. Another issue, of course is the extent to which cultural or historical perspectives in these two countries distinguish them from other countries and explain their "outlier" status on happiness scores. While this perspective is an important one, elaborating upon it would require an additional chapter at least. We thank an anonymous reviewer for raising this point.

4. Pritchett, Suryahadi, and Sumarto (2000) define "vulnerability" as a probability: the risk that a household will experience at least one episode of poverty in the near future. They set a threshold level of .5, so that a household is vulnerable if its odds of falling into poverty are 50-50 or worse. In a 1997–2000 study of Indonesian households, they found that even though the poverty line was 20 percent at any given point in time, as many as 50 percent of all households were vulnerable—that is, fell into poverty at some point—during the three-year period.

5. For detail, see the chapter on Peru in Graham (1994).

1994, making Peru the fastest growing economy in the world. A consequent effort was made to increase social expenditures, particularly for the extremely poor. In the mid- and late 1990s, the growth trajectory was more mixed. For the decade the country's overall growth averaged 4.2 percent, which was the third best performance on the continent, after Chile and Mexico.[6] As a result, a significant number of Peruvians escaped poverty during the 1990s. Yet a similar number of people fell into poverty at some point. The people most vulnerable to falling into poverty tended to be not the poorest workers, but rather the workers who were most integrated into the formal economy and whose wages were most vulnerable to shock-related fluctuations.[7] This vulnerability to falling into poverty also affected reported well-being.

In Russia a deep economic recession persisted throughout the 1990s, making downward mobility into poverty the norm, rather than the exception, for large numbers of people. Poverty increased at an unprecedented rate. In both Peru and Russia, high rates of mobility and volatility were coupled with the globalization of consumption standards and a scaling back of public social insurance.

As discussed in chapter 3, inequality as measured by the Gini increased from the mid-1980s to early 1990s, particularly for Russia. For Peru, as for other strong market reformers in Latin America, it decreased slightly.[8] Polarization—defined as a thinning of the middle of the distribution vis-à-vis the bottom tail—first fell markedly in Peru 1990–94 and then increased slightly from 1994–97. Middle-income stress (MIS), our measure that captures the income share of the top versus that of the middle, displayed similar trends. In Russia, where reforms were far less complete, increases in polarization and in MIS were significant.[9] Yet the picture provided by all of these measures is still incomplete. Shorter-term movements up and down the income ladder, which these measures do not capture, may have the most effects on perceptions of well-being.

6. ECLAC (2000).
7. With capital mobility, macroeconomic risk gets shifted onto domestic factors of production that are immobile, such as workers in the formal sector; see Rodrik (1999).
8. For detail, see Birdsall, Graham, and Pettinato (2000).
9. For detail on the limited nature of the reforms in Russia, see Gaddy and Ickes (1998).

Panel Data Evidence from Peru

Measuring dynamic trends in inequality, or income mobility, requires panel data.[10] Yet panel data—as well as sound data on perceptions—are scarce in the developing economies. We have both kinds of data for Peru and Russia, and those data reveal a tremendous amount of movement up and down the income ladder.[11] This suggests that many people in these countries—particularly those in the middle—experience vast fluctuations in economic welfare, with consequent effects on perceptions of well-being. In Peru we were able to collaborate with the Instituto Cuánto to reinterview a subset of households that had participated in a 1985–2000 nationally representative panel and thus were able to compare respondents' subjective assessments of their well-being with objective trends.[12] The study was conducted in 1998, 1999, and 2000.[13] For the year 2000, we increased the panel from 152 households to 500 households, both to increase the sample size and to avoid the attrition bias that could result from such a long panel.[14] The additional households are in a panel that began in 1991 (table 5-1). Thus for the 500-household sample, we have objective data for 1991 through 2000 and subjective data for 2000.[15] Household income levels for the panel are, on average, slightly higher than those of the nationally representative sample.

A note of caution is necessary when interpreting change data from all longitudinal surveys. One problem is attrition: those on the extreme tails of the

10. For a summary of new economics research in this area, see Birdsall and Graham (2000).

11. Whereas the studies of the United States and Europe have constructed cohort national panels, our data for Peru and Russia actually follow the same individuals across time.

12. A full national sample was not possible for the panel studies in the early 1990s, because guerrillas controlled some areas of the country. The perceptions study involved the collaboration of Nancy Birdsall, Carol Graham, and Richard Webb of Cuánto S.A. and was undertaken with funds from the Inter-American Development Bank, Brookings Center on Social and Economic Dynamics, and the MacArthur and Tinker Foundations.

13. The results of the 1998 pilot survey are described in greater detail in Webb (2000); the 1999 survey results are in Graham and Pettinato (2000).

14. Carter and May (1999), among others, find that attrition bias tends to be at the tails of the distribution, which is not surprising; it suggests that poor households that cannot "make it" move away, as do those who "strike it rich." By adding more than double the original number of households—with the new ones from a shorter panel—we sought to eliminate as much of this attrition bias as possible.

15. The full panel study was repeated in 1985, 1990, 1991, 1994, 1996, 1997, and 2000. The 2000 perceptions study coincided with the full panel study, which allowed us to update the objective data.

Table 5-1. *Household Panel Summary Information, Peru, 2000*

Variable	Frequency	Mean	Standard deviation	Minimum	Maximum
Age	500	52.95	15.29	18	93
Gender (male = 1)	500	0.53	0.50	0	1
Household expenditures[a]	500	18,892	14,544	2,790	132,202
Household members	500	4.98	2.21	1	14
Years of education	500	8.02	4.66	0	18
Area (urban = 1)	500	0.86	0.35	0	1

Source: Authors' calculations based on 2000 Peru survey conducted by the authors in conjunction with the Instituto Cuanto in Peru.

a. In soles, as of August 2000; U.S. $1 = 3.48 soles.

distribution are the most likely to drop out of the panel, as the wealthiest may move to better neighborhoods and the poorest who "don't make it" may move in with other family members or opt for other kinds of coping strategies. Thus panels can be biased in their representation of all income groups. The second problem, measurement error, involves possible error stemming from the difficulty of accurately measuring the incomes of those individuals who work in the informal economy or in the agricultural sector. Although we cannot discount the possible presence of some errors of these kinds, our data are based on expenditures, rather than income, a practice that tends to reduce this kind of measurement error. The data are also adjusted to Lima 2000 prices to account for regional and rural-urban differences.

The perceptions questionnaire addressed perceptions of and satisfaction with changes in the household's economic welfare over the last ten to fifteen years; perceptions and changes in the availability and quality of public services used by the household (health, schools, security, water, sanitation, and municipal government); respondents' assessments of future economic prospects; and the respondents' participation in community organizations.[16]

16. Because the literature shows that negative health shocks can have negative effects on mobility as well as happiness, the questionnaire originally had questions about health. Yet problems in the definition of health victims and differences among individual respondents' interpretations of the health questions led us to drop them, at least for this stage of the research. For effects of health on mobility, see Deaton and Paxson (1994); for effects of health on happiness, see Diener (1984) and Frey and Stutzer (1999).

Perceived past mobility was based on a question asking respondents to compare the economic situation of their household with its situation ten to fifteen years earlier. The possible responses were: much worse, worse, same, better, much better. Other questions in the survey asked respondents to compare their family's current job situation with that of ten to fifteen years earlier, to compare their economic situation with that of their parents at the same point in their lives, and to state their degree of satisfaction with their standard of living.

As explained in chapter 3, our Markov transition matrix for Peru shows substantial mobility—both upward and downward (see table 3-2). Those in the third and fourth quintiles clearly experienced the most downward mobility, while those in the first and second quintiles (the poorest) experienced the most—and the most intense—upward mobility, with a significant proportion of these moving up two or even three quintiles.[17] Among other things, these trends reflect the benefits to the poor of stabilizing hyperinflation, the government's targeting of public expenditures to the poorest groups, and changes in opportunity generated by the high economic growth after inflation was stabilized.

In terms of absolute mobility, the majority of households in the panel— 58 percent—had income increases of 30 percent or more from 1991 through 2000.[18] Thirty percent experienced only marginal income changes, and 12 percent had income drops of 30 percent or more. Analyzing these changes logarithmically (a measure that reflects the greater proportional importance of changes in income for those with lower levels of income), we find that the mobility trends had greater significance for those at the bottom end of the income ladder. For example the positive changes that occurred from 1996 through 2000 were more significant for households in the lower

17. A comparison of these movements with data from the United States highlights their extremity. U.S. Census data show that 81.6 percent of those families who were in the bottom quintile of the income distribution in 1985 were still there the next year, while the fraction that remained in the top quintile for that period was 76.3 percent. About half the families that start in either the top or bottom quintile of the income distribution are still there after a decade, and only 3 to 6 percent rise from the bottom to the top or fall from top to bottom; see Krugman (1992).

18. Income changes are measured on the basis of household expenditure data in Lima 2000 prices, adjusted for household size using a one-parameter equivalence scale with elasticity of 0.5. For details on the implications in using this or other equivalence methods, see Figini (1998).

part of the distribution. Trends in measured poverty support this: extreme poverty fell between 1994 and 2000, while nonextreme poverty increased.[19] In contrast to these positive objective results, however, there was a negative skew on perceptions. Forty-five percent of households had very negative or negative views of their own economic experiences, while 24 percent were indifferent and 31 percent were positive.

The asymmetry between reported income changes and perceived economic status was even more marked in the 1998 survey, when the period over which income was measured was longer (1985–1997); in addition the objective data on income change were from 1997, which meant that the period over which individuals had to recall their economic progress was longer, introducing a higher margin of measurement error. Fifty-eight percent of households had negative views, 28 percent were indifferent and 12 percent were positive. We attribute this difference to recall problems, as well as to what we term a time-log effect. In other words, any given income gain will have more impact on perceptions if it occurs over a shorter period of time, say six years (1994–2000) rather than twelve years (1985–97).

The negative skew on economic assessments contrasts with a fairly positive one on self-assessments of housing improvements: in the 2000 survey 44 percent of respondents said that their housing quality was better than it was ten years earlier, whereas only 14 percent said it was worse. This may reflect the difficulty in making accurate economic assessments over time, particularly for the self-employed who do not earn regular wages. Housing changes are more concrete in nature.[20]

Those with the most absolute expenditure gains show a strong negative skew on perceptions of economic progress despite their favorable economic performance. Of the high performers in the sample (those with expenditure improvements of 30 percent or more from 1991 through 2000), 43 percent said they were worse off and only 30 percent said their situation was better. Of

19. The extreme poverty measure is based on the number of individuals unable to meet basic food needs. The poverty line is based on essential food needs as well as an additional basket of household needs. We discuss this measure in chapter 3, footnote 14; see also Fields and Ok (1999).

20. Assessments of the state of public services were even more optimistic: 55 percent of respondents said the state of public education was better, 19 percent said worse; 54 percent said access to water and electric services was better, while 13 percent said it was worse, reflecting substantial government efforts to make improvements in this arena.

Table 5-2. *Long-Term Perceived Mobility versus Objective Income Mobility, Peru, 2000*

Perceived mobility 1991–2000	Objective mobility 1991–2000 (% income change)			
	100+	99 to 30	30 to –30	–30 to less
Very negative	19.0	19.4	19.3	20.7
Negative	23.9	24.0	25.3	36.2
Indifferent	24.5	27.9	22.7	19.0
Positive	26.4	26.4	27.3	19.0
Very positive	6.1	2.3	5.3	5.2
Total	100.0	100.0	100.0	100.0

Source: Authors' calculations based on 2000 Peru survey conducted by the authors in conjunction with the Instituto Cuanto in Peru.

the worst performers (those with declines of 30 percent or more), 57 percent stated, accurately, that they were worse off; 21 percent said that their situation had not changed, and 24 percent saw themselves as better off (table 5-2).

Our regression analysis of the determinants of perceived past mobility found that many of the demographic variables—gender, education, and marital status—did not have significant effects (table 5-3). Age has a significant and negative correlation with perceived past mobility, without the quadratic effect usually found on perceptions variables. In other words, assessments of past mobility become monotonically less positive with age and do not have the U-shaped quality—first a decrease in optimism or happiness and then an increase—found in studies of both past progress and happiness for our larger, regional sample. Living in an urban area had a negative and significant correlation with past perceived mobility, whereas income level (as measured by log of equivalent expenditure) had a positive and significant correlation.

Income change, meanwhile, when measured by changes in log expenditure, had no effects on perceived past mobility when changes over the 1991–2000 time period were used, but had a positive and significant correlation when changes over a shorter time period, 1994–2000, were used. This is most likely due to recall problems, as well as to the possible time-log effect noted earlier: the same percentage change in income has more impact if it occurs in a shorter period of time (see table 5-3). The results also suggest that these income changes had stronger effects for those at the lower end of

Table 5-3. *Perceived Past Mobility, Peru, 2000*[a]

Independent variable	1	2	3
Age	−0.026	−0.023	−0.023
	(−4.771)	(−4.302)	(−4.336)
Male dummy	−0.190	−0.163	−0.185
	(−1.090)	(−0.935)	(−1.062)
Education	0.003	0.022	0.021
	(0.178)	(1.204)	(1.154)
Married	0.119	0.086	0.118
	(0.694)	(0.506)	(0.686)
Urban	−0.664	−0.494	−0.454
	(−2.801)	(−2.142)	(−1.969)
Log expenditure	0.420	. . .	. . .
	(2.772)		
Mobility 1991–2000	. . .	0.789	. . .
		(0.754)	
Mobility 1994–2000	. . .	. . .	2.647
			(2.205)
Number of observations	500	500	500
Pseudo R^2	(0.024)	(0.020)	(0.023)

Source: Authors' calculations based on 2000 Peru survey conducted by the authors in conjunction with the Instituto Cuanto in Peru.
a. Ordered logit estimations. *z* statistics are in parentheses.

the income ladder.[21] In a related finding, short-term fluctuations in income (as opposed to income levels) had stronger effects on the subjective assessments of the poor than of wealthier groups, because the former have less of a margin to absorb such fluctuations.[22]

Relative income differences are, no doubt, influencing these assessments of well-being, as Easterlin found in his studies. Forces other than income

21. There were no significant results on PPM when we used changes in equivalence expenditure, rather than log expenditure, for the same time period (1994–2000).
22. In an ordered logit estimation with economic satisfaction as the dependent variable, we find that mean adjusted expenditure for 1991–2000 (a long-term measure of income) has positive and significant effects on economic satisfaction, while in the same estimation, expenditure per capita for 2000 (a short-term level) is insignificant. When we use the log of both these expenditure measures, which highlights the impact of these trends for those with less income, we find that the mean over time is insignificant, while expenditure levels for 2000 are positive and significant. This suggests that short-term changes in income levels have more impact on the poor, while longer-term income is more relevant for wealthier groups, who can better absorb short-term fluctuations.

may also be at play. Hirschman noted many years ago that "the economist, with his touching simplicity, would tend to think there was no problem [for the upwardly mobile]: being better off than before, these people are also likely to be more content . . . , [yet] social history has shown . . . that matters are far more complicated."[23] Even though the upwardly mobile might have advanced in income terms, other obstacles, rigidities, and discriminatory practices might still block their continued ascent, particularly along nonincome dimensions, thus preventing them from feeling as though they had really "made it."

The differences in responses also result from cultural differences, as well as from higher expectations and more experience answering surveys among urban respondents. As in the earlier surveys, in the year 2000 urban (and more educated) respondents were more likely to give extreme responses ("much worse" rather than "worse," for example) than were rural ones. Among upwardly mobile respondents—those that had income gains of 30 percent or more—49 percent of urban respondents assessed their past progress negatively, while only 20 percent of rural respondents did so. In contrast, 51 percent of upwardly mobile rural respondents said their situation was the same, while only 21 percent of urban ones did so. Our "frustrated achievers"—defined as those respondents who were upwardly mobile from 1991 through 2000, but whose perceived past mobility was negative— are clearly more prevalent in urban areas (table 5-4).

Analyzing the sample by income group, we find that the negative skew in perceptions is higher for the middle quintile than for either poorer or richer respondents.[24] Fifty-one percent of the upwardly mobile in the middle, or third, quintile assessed their past economic progress as negative or very negative, compared with 36 percent in the first quintile, 45 percent in the second, 43 percent in the fourth, and 45 percent in the fifth.[25] Poor respondents

23. Hirschman (1973, pp. 550–51).

24. Measurement error might also account for some of these differences, although it is much more common to find reporting errors at the tails of the distribution, rather than at the middle. In addition, because the survey relies on expenditure rather than income data, it avoids some of the difficulties entailed in measuring income in the context of high levels of inflation, as well as of individuals who do not have fixed salaries, such as most informal sector workers. All reported expenditures were deflated to Lima 2000 prices.

25. Our quintiles are constructed on the basis of the respondents in the panel, using household expenditure, adjusted for household size considering economies of scale (see chap-

Table 5-4. *Frustrated Achievers in Peru, 2000*

	Mean			
Variable	Whole sample	Frustrated achievers	Non-frustrated achievers	Differ-ence[a]
Age	52.95 (15.29)	55.67 (15.09)	49.49 (14.90)	**
Area (urban = 1)	0.86 (0.35)	0.93 (0.26)	0.78 (0.42)	***
Gender (male = 1)	0.53 (0.50)	0.51 (0.50)	0.57 (0.50)	. . .
Education	8.02 (4.66)	8.03 (4.52)	8.12 (4.68)	. . .
Equivalence household expenditure (2000)	8,922 (7,314)	9,885 (6,144)	9,957 (10,809)	. . .
Coefficient of variation (1991, 1994, 1996, 2000)	0.42 (0.19)	0.43 (0.19)	0.48 (0.19)	**
Economic satisfaction	2.91 (0.80)	2.53 (0.78)	3.21 (0.64)	**
Job satisfaction	2.58 (1.16)	1.88 (0.90)	3.15 (1.03)	*
Perception of economic opportunity	3.03 (0.75)	2.74 (0.71)	3.28 (0.65)	*
Economic ladder question	3.82 (1.52)	3.73 (1.47)	3.98 (1.59)	***
Prospect of upward mobility	3.29 (1.03)	3.03 (1.13)	3.54 (0.89)	**

Source: Authors' calculations based on 2000 Peru survey conducted by authors in conjunction with the Instituto Cuanto in Peru. Standard deviations are in parentheses.

a. Difference of the means between frustrated achievers and nonfrustrated achievers; * significant at the 1 percent level, ** significant at the 5 percent level, *** significant at the 10 percent level.

were much more likely than wealthy ones to say their situation had not changed: 41 percent of those in the first quintile answered "same," compared with only 19 percent of those in the fifth quintile (figure 5-1). This

ter 3, note 13). These quintiles are not the same as national income quintiles, as the households in our panel were, on average, slightly wealthier than those in the nationally representative sample.

Figure 5-1. *Perceived Past Mobility among Upwardly Mobile, Peru, 1991–2000*

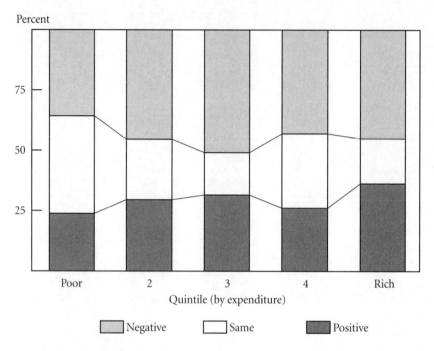

Source: Authors' calculations, based on Peru survey conducted in 2000 by authors in conjunction with the Instituto Cuanto in Peru.

finding supports our earlier point that poor—particularly poor rural—respondents are less likely to opt for extreme responses and have lower reference norms.

Economic trends in Peru have played out differently among income groups, as they have in most emerging market countries. The wealthy have benefited and will continue to benefit from the rewards that the market is yielding for skills and education, while the poor have benefited from a significant expansion of transfers and public expenditures.[26] Rewards for those in the middle have varied, depending on their skill and education levels. People in the middle are also more likely to view the wealthy as a reference group than are the very poor. Thus if those in the middle are—or perceive

26. See Graham and Kane (1998); World Bank (1999).

that they are—very far from reaching the status of their reference group, they may be quite frustrated, even though they are advancing up the economic ladder.[27] Our results suggest that these differences lead to the middle-income stress discussed in an earlier chapter. In contrast, absolute income gains among the poorest sectors have a consistent and positive impact on life satisfaction.[28]

Frustrated Achievers in Peru

Looking more closely at our Peruvian frustrated achievers, we find that their mean education and expenditure levels are virtually the same as those of their nonfrustrated counterparts. Rather surprisingly the frustrated achievers experience *less* volatility in income than the nonfrustrated group.[29] Yet despite the absence of major income differences, the frustrated achievers had much lower scores on virtually all of our perceptions variables. Frustrated achievers had lower mean POUM scores and much lower mean scores on questions dealing with economic satisfaction, job satisfaction, and "prospects for improving future standard of living" (see table 5-4).

On average, the frustrated achievers were seven years older (56) than the nonfrustrated group (49)—a statistically significant difference—and age or life cycle effects may have a role in explaining their negative perceptions. Van Praag and colleagues, for example, find that middle-age respondents give greater weight to present and anticipated income than do either the young or the old, who place greater importance on past income.[30] Middle-age respondents are more likely to have immediate expenditure needs because they are likely to have more dependents than either the young or the old and because they are better able to estimate their future incomes than are younger respondents who have not yet established an earnings trajectory.

27. Hirschman's "tunnel effect" may also be at play here.
28. *Happiness* levels clearly show a log relationship with income. The decreasing impact on happiness of a marginal increase in income supports microeconomic diminishing returns assumptions. At very high levels of income, some studies find that the curve becomes convex—perhaps reflecting greed?
29. This was measured by the coefficient of variation, defined as the standard deviation for each household divided by its mean expenditure levels for the 1991–2000 period. The coefficient for Russia was significantly higher for the frustrated than for the nonfrustrated group, meanwhile. Data for Russia are income rather than expenditure based, and the former vary more.
30. Van Praag and Frijters (1999).

Table 5-5. *Economic Satisfaction, Peru, 2000*[a]

Independent variable	Coefficient
Age	−0.013
	(−2.132)
Male dummy	0.160
	(0.826)
Education	0.033
	(1.533)
Married	0.009
	(0.046)
Urban	−0.830
	(−3.096)
Log expenditure	0.756
	(4.452)
Number of observations	500
Pseudo R^2	0.036

Source: Authors' calculations, based on 2000 Peru survey conducted by authors in conjunction with the Instituto Cuanto in Peru.

a. Ordered logit estimation. *z* statistics are in parentheses.

Frustrated achievers may also be working more hours for the income gains that they make. Although we do not have information on hours worked (nor is there any available from any other data set we are aware of), one could imagine that if gains came at high costs in terms of sacrificed leisure, they might also be accompanied by frustration. This might also be more relevant for older respondents, who tend to value leisure more.

Our regressions on the Peru sample as a whole found a significant and negative relationship between age and perceived past mobility and between age and economic satisfaction (see tables 5-3 and 5-5). Neither perceived past mobility nor economic satisfaction produced the usual quadratic relation with age. In larger samples life satisfaction usually first decreases with age and then increases monotonically at a certain point: somewhere in the mid-forties for the advanced industrial economies and Latin America and slightly later for Russia.[31] The nonquadratic relationship found in Peru may be explained by small sample size or by the slightly different phrasing of the

31. See Blanchflower and Oswald (1999) for the advanced industrial economies; Graham and Pettinato (2001) for Latin America.

question in Peru, which is "How satisfied are you with your present standard of living?" rather than the usual "How satisfied are you with your life?" The economic element in the question may dominate the usual demographic effects on life satisfaction.

We also found that job satisfaction was downward-sloping with age. The primary determinants of job satisfaction in Peru were log expenditure and age. Education levels were insignificant, which supports the findings of other studies of job satisfaction in the advanced industrial countries.[32]

The negative skew on perceptions was not as evident in respondents' evaluations of their satisfaction with their current standard of living. Only 23 percent of respondents evaluated their current standard of living as "bad" or "very bad," whereas 58 percent said it was "regular," and 19 percent said it was "good" or "very good." More than two-thirds of the households (68 percent) were confident that their children would do better than they; only 14 percent thought their children would do worse. Future expectations, even more than subjective assessments, are affected by noneconomic factors such as hope and determination. In contrast, however, only 21 percent of respondents thought that they lived better than their parents had, while 61 percent thought that their parents had lived better than they did.

Respondents were also asked to assess their opportunities to improve their standard of living in the future, as well as how their opportunities compared with those their parents had and that their children would have. Seventeen percent thought that their future opportunities for improvement were bad or very bad, 61 percent thought they were regular, and 22 percent thought they were good or very good. A striking 49 percent thought that their parents had had better opportunities to enhance their standard of living, 22 percent felt they had the same chances, and 29 percent felt they had greater opportunities than their parents. Expectations for children remained higher, however: 59 percent expected their children to have greater opportunities, and only 13 percent thought that their children would have fewer opportunities.

---

32. On job satisfaction in Britain, see Clark and Oswald (1996). It is not difficult to imagine that the effects of education on job satisfaction are mixed, as in many cases, people may either be overqualified for their jobs or perceive that they are. In Peru in the late 1990s, meanwhile, as in much of Latin America, rewards to secondary school completion were diminishing with respect to rewards to either primary or higher education; see Birdsall, Graham, and Pettinato (2000).

An outstanding question is what these negative perceptions imply for future economic and political behavior. We cannot answer this definitively, but some of our results are suggestive. Using the regionwide Latinobarometro data and controlling for other variables, we find that having a positive assessment of one's present economic situation compared with one's past situation has a positive (and significant) correlation with happiness, suggesting that frustrated achievers are less happy than other respondents.[33] Similarly, for our Peru sample, having positive perceptions of past mobility was correlated positively with economic satisfaction. Our analysis of data from Russia, discussed later, yields a similar correlation between perceived past mobility and happiness.[34]

Recent theoretical research on ego and identity suggests that assessing one's situation positively can lead to a bias in processing information, in which individuals reject or ignore information that could change their positive self-image. Those with negative self-images, meanwhile, are more likely to seek out new information and to take risks.[35] With this logic, one could posit that the frustrated achievers would continue to seek out new opportunities, despite their negative assessments of the past. In contrast, much of the research that has been done on reference groups would suggest a much less optimistic interpretation of how the frustrations of the achievers might influence future economic behavior.

Reference Groups

In 1949 Duesenberry discussed the relationship between income aspirations and social status, and its influence on savings behavior. He referred to sociological research in the United States in the 1940s, which found that people who associated with others who had more income than they had tended to be less satisfied with their income than were people who associated with others who were at the same income level.[36]

---

33. The phrasing of the question in the Peru survey was slightly different: "how satisfied are you with your current standard of living?" In the Latinobarometro and the RLMS the question was "how satisfied are you with your life?"

34. Having a pro-market attitude also has a similar strong, positive, and consistent effect on happiness. We discuss this in detail in Graham and Pettinato (2001).

35. Koszegi (2000).

36. Duesenberry (1949).

More recent empirical research on savings suggests that having a higher reference norm or comparison income can lead to conspicuous consumption and lower savings rates. A study in the Netherlands, for example, finds that, on average, more educated and wealthier people save more. Yet controlling for income and education, those who have wealthier friends and neighbors save less.[37] A plausible explanation is that those who live in more expensive neighborhoods are both spending more and tend to know their neighbors. Or perhaps those who want to keep up with the Joneses know more rich Joneses and also save less because of behavioral traits.[38] Whatever the reason, instead of saving, frustrated achievers may be opting for immediate consumption to "keep up with" the reference groups they aspire to. Immediate consumption could also be motivated by the wide availability of imported consumer goods.

In an effort to find some insights into the effects of frustration on future behavior, we theorized that our frustrated achievers and our nonfrustrated ones might have different reference groups. For the year 2000 survey, we included an economic ladder question (ELQ) similar to one used in other surveys to gauge the influence of reference norms, that is, how people compare themselves to others in their country. The question here was phrased: "on a ladder of nine steps, where the poorest are on the first step and the richest are on the ninth step, where would you place yourself?" At our request, a similar question, asking people to rank themselves on a ten-step ladder, was also included in the 2000 version of the regionwide Latinobarometro survey.[39]

The Latinobarometro results show the majority of respondents placing themselves in the middle categories, even if they are slightly above or below them according to an objective index of wealth. Average ELQ responses for those in the lowest income decile were 3.4, just above the third rung of the ladder, while average responses for those in the wealthiest decile were 5.3,

37. See Kapteyn (2000). For theoretical work on conspicuous consumption, see Robson (1992) and Cole, Mailath, and Postlewaite (1995). On reference norms and saving, see Carroll (1994).

38. Once again, we are grateful to George Akerlof for elaborating this point further than we originally had.

39. Unfortunately, our estimated wealth data for the Latinobarometro survey is much less precise than the expenditure data we have for Peru.

Figure 5-2. *Mean Responses on Economic Ladder Question, Peru, 2000*

Mean response

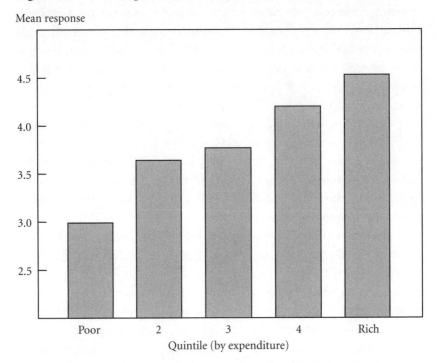

Quintile (by expenditure)

Source: Authors' calculations, based on Peru survey conducted in 2000 by authors in conjunction with the Instituto Cuanto in Peru.

just above the middle of the ladder. In Peru mean responses were 3.0 for the lowest quintile and 4.5 for the wealthiest. This regression toward the mean suggests that reference norms are at play, as in much of the other literature on happiness. We also note a very slight flattening on the upward curve at quintile three in Peru, suggesting a higher comparison group for those in the middle of the distribution (figure 5-2). The mean ELQ responses by decile for Latin America show a fairly even monotonic increase (figure 5-3).

For Peru years of education, being married, and wealth levels (log expenditure) are all positively correlated with ELQ responses. Rather surprisingly, age and changes in income (regardless of whether they are measured using changes in logs) are insignificant, as is the urban dummy, after controlling for income levels (table 5-6). A similar positive correlation of ELQ responses with education, wealth, and marital status appears for the

Figure 5-3. *Mean Responses on Economic Ladder Question, by Decile, in Latin America, 2000*

Mean response

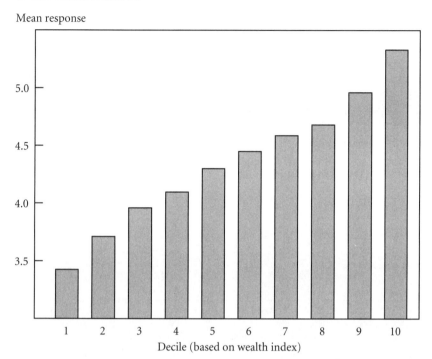

Decile (based on wealth index)

Source: Authors' calculations, based on the Latinobarometro Survey for 2000.

Latin America sample. We also get a quadratic age effect for the Latin America sample.[40]

Meanwhile, the frustrated achievers in Peru have slightly lower mean ELQ scores than do their nonfrustrated counterparts. We also explored differences in respondents' evaluations of their economic situation over the past ten years relative, first, to their community and then to their country. Overall, people were more optimistic when they assessed themselves relative to their community than their country. Only 15 percent said they had fared worse than others in their community, while 23 said they had fared worse than others in their country; 27 percent said that they had fared better than

40. The difference here may be explained by the difference in sample size: the 17,000 observations in Latinobarometro probably capture whatever age effects there are better than do the 500 observations in Peru.

Table 5-6. *Economic Ladder Question, Peru, 2000*[a]

Independent variable	1	2
Age	0.000	0.004
	(−0.101)	(0.836)
Male dummy	−0.166	−0.138
	(−1.201)	(−0.965)
Education	0.032	0.070
	(2.066)	(4.667)
Married	0.290	0.239
	(2.124)	(1.687)
Urban	0.179	0.429
	(0.900)	(2.115)
Log expenditure	0.748	. . .
	(6.293)	
1991–2000 mobility	. . .	0.171
		(0.196)
Constant	−3.291	2.630
	(−3.329)	(8.335)
Number of observations	500	500
R^2	0.142	0.074

Source: Authors' calculations, based on 2000 Peru survey conducted by authors in conjunction with the Instituto Cuanto in Peru.

a. Ordinary least squares regression. *t* statistics are in parentheses.

those in their community, while only 15 percent said they had fared better than those in their country.

These results suggest that reference norms at the community level are lower than those outside the community. It seems plausible, therefore, that the frustrations of our achievers are driven by national (and possibly global) rather than by community-level trends, particularly as the difference between community level and national level assessments of upwardly mobile respondents was remarkably similar to that for the sample as a whole.[41]

Interestingly, our frustrated achievers (those with upward mobility but negative assessments of that mobility) were much more negative in their

41. The results of our regression analysis to identify the determinants of these responses were disappointing and inconsistent. Years of education was the only variable that was significant and positively correlated to responding that one had done better than one's community. Income mobility (change in log expenditure from 1994 to 2000) was the only significant variable (positive) for assessments vis-à-vis the country.

Table 5-7. *Frustrated Achievers and Reference Groups, Peru, 2000*

Personal situation compared to ...	Frustrated achievers	Nonfrustrated achievers	Total
... the rest of your local community			
Worse	23.4	8.1	14.9
Same	61.7	55.0	58.0
Better	14.9	36.9	27.1
Total	100.0	100.0	100.0
... the rest of your country			
Worse	33.6	13.7	22.6
Same	57.0	66.3	62.1
Better	9.4	20.0	15.3
Total	100.0	100.0	100.0

Source: Authors' calculations, based on 2000 Peru survey conducted by authors in conjunction with the Instituto Cuanto in Peru.

comparisons to their respective reference groups than were the nonfrustrated upwardly mobile respondents. Far fewer frustrated achievers (15 percent said that they had done *better* than those in their community than did nonfrustrated achievers (37 percent). Similarly, a far smaller percentage of frustrated (9 percent) than nonfrustrated achievers (20.0 percent) believed that they had done better than those in their country (table 5-7).

MAD: British and American Style

We developed two additional variables, based on the Peru data, that suggest the existence of differences between perceptions about economic *change* and those about economic *status*. The mobility assessment discrepancy (MAD) is the ratio between subjective and objective income mobility.[42] When MAD is equal to 1, the respondent is perceiving his or her actual mobility accurately. A MAD ratio greater than 1 (>1) implies that the respondent assesses the situation more positively than it actually is, and is "mad" in the British sense, that is, a Pollyanna. A MAD ratio lower than 1 (<1) suggests the respondent is "mad" or frustrated in the American sense of the word.

42. This was a ratio between PPM responses (five possible categories) and objective "mobility quintiles," which were defined according to percentage expenditure mobility in 1991–2000. We have not corrected for standard bias.

The perceptions gap (PG) is the ratio between a respondent's ELQ response and his or her actual income decile. A high PG suggests that the perception has overstated the actual income status; a low PG suggests the opposite. When these perceptions variables are applied to the frustrated achiever category in Peru, we find that they have, on average, lower PG ratios, reflecting their tendency to place themselves lower on the economic ladder than they actually are.

Our regressions with the perceptions gap as the dependent variable yield significant and negative effects for age (nonquadratic), education, and living in an urban area. This latter finding is not surprising, as reference norms are higher in urban than in rural areas. The only significant coefficient on MAD, meanwhile, was age, which came in strong and negative, supporting other findings that frustration increases monotonically with age for our sample.

The perceptions gap seems more sensitive to stable norms and reference groups than does the MAD, which is driven by changes (and perceived changes) in status. We also looked at mean MAD responses by income quintile, that is, how perceptions accord with actual trends in absolute income, and how, or if, discrepancies vary according to where the respondent actually is in the income distribution. The correlation for the MAD is negative, with mean responses lower (therefore reflecting greater frustration) for the top quintiles. This suggests that the MAD is affected by people shifting their norms upward with gains in income, making the MAD appear to be a more sensitive variable to income dynamics than is the PG.

Social Capital

We included several questions in our Peru survey about participation in community organizations and reasons for participating. We initially hypothesized that the concept of social capital needs to be disaggregated to reflect the many different reasons that people associate, particularly the safety net and joint survival nature of many of the neighborhood organizations that the poor join. We then asked respondents if they participated in community organizations (roughly 60 percent said they participated in one or more organizations), and if so, in how many, with a long list of the possible organizations that they might belong to. A second question asked respondents why they participated, with the four possible answers being economic benefit, receipt of emergency aid (including food), recreation and leisure, and new relations and contacts. We then created two new variables that, for each individual, enumerated participation in organizations by reason for participating: economic (the first two answers) and noneconomic (the second two answers).[43]

When we regressed the nondisaggregated participation variable on income mobility, controlling for a number of other variables, in an attempt to see if participation was a plausible explanatory variable for upward mobility, we had no significant results. We also had no significant results when we used participation as the dependent variable, and, in order to determine the reasons for participating, used either mobility or income level (both 1991 and 2000 income levels in separate regressions) as independent variables (column 1 of table 5-8).

In contrast, when we disaggregated the participation variable and regressed participating for noneconomic reasons on income mobility, to see if this kind of participation was a plausible explanatory variable, we found a positive and significant correlation (columns 2 and 3 of table 5-8). When we did the reverse exercise to explore the determinants of participation and regressed mobility (log income mobility) on participating for noneconomic reasons—controlling for demographic variables as well as for occupation groups—we found a positive and significant relationship. Substituting 2000 equivalence income for income mobility as an explanatory variable, we also got a positive and significant coefficient, but it was not nearly as strong.

When we repeated the same set of regressions, using participating for economic necessity reasons instead of for noneconomic reasons, we found no significant relationship with either mobility or income levels. We did find that years of education was significant and negatively correlated with participating for economic reasons. This is no surprise, given that more education is linked to better occupational opportunities, and more educated people are less likely to need safety nets or other group economic survival strategies.

We also found that being married was significantly and negatively correlated with both kinds of participation, which is not surprising given that the

43. Of those 296 individuals in the sample that participated in at least one organization, 59 percent participated in organizations for economic reasons, while 75 percent participated in organizations for noneconomic reasons. Note that individuals could have different reasons for participating in each organization to which they belonged.

Table 5-8. *Mobility and Participation, Peru, 2000*[a]

Independent variable	1	2	3
Age	0.000	0.000	0.000
	(−1.381)	(−1.571)	(−1.288)
Male dummy	0.005	0.005	0.004
	(0.658)	(0.681)	(0.553)
Education	0.001	0.001	0.001
	(1.695)	(1.547)	(1.641)
Married	−0.005	−0.006	−0.004
	(−0.665)	(−0.826)	(−0.537)
Urban	−0.014	−0.016	−0.014
	(−1.3730	(−1.548)	(−1.328)
Participation (general)	0.002	...	...
	(0.903)		
Participation for economic reasons	...	−0.002	...
		(−0.637)	
Participation for noneconomic reasons	...	...	0.007
			(2.169)
Constant	0.063	0.072	0.058
	(3.621)	(4.265)	(3.503)
Number of observations	500	500	500
R^2	0.018	0.018	0.026

Source: Authors' calculations based on 2000 Peru survey conducted by authors in conjunction with the Instituto Cuanto in Peru.

a. Ordinary least squares regression. *t* statistics are in parentheses.

opportunity costs of time are higher for those with families. (An alternative explanation is, of course, that people participate in these organizations because they are lonely and looking for a partner.)

A related finding is that our frustrated achievers were *less* likely to participate in organizations for noneconomic reasons than were the nonfrustrated achievers. The participation rate in organizations for economic reasons was about the same for the two groups (and was slightly lower than for participation for noneconomic reasons).[44]

These findings, while perhaps limited in their significance by the size of the sample, are remarkably supportive of Granovetter's work on the strength of weak ties. As described in chapter 2, Granovetter contends—

44. *T* tests for significance showed a significant difference between mean participation rates on participation for noneconomic reasons. Results are available from the authors.

and shows empirically based on data on the promotion records of blue- and white-collar workers in the United States—that it is "weak ties," or associations outside the individual's close-knit network, that are key to upward mobility, rather than the close friendships and neighborhood groups that he classifies as "strong ties."

Much of the literature on social capital, however, aggregates all kinds of organizations, or focuses on close-knit neighborhood or kinship groups.[45] Our economic associations are much more like strong ties, which provide safety nets in times of need but do not provide ties outside the group or new opportunities for employment. Our noneconomic associations are more likely to provide new acquaintances and ties beyond the close network; indeed that is one of the stated reasons for joining such organizations. (It may also be the case, of course, that more successful people are more likely to be invited to join such groups, and that the causality runs in the other direction. In the case of the organizations that we looked at in Peru, however, association is voluntary and not by invitation.)

Our findings are also in keeping with theoretical work of both Karla Hoff and Steven Durlauf, who demonstrate how some of the group survival organizations of the poor, while providing critical safety net support, can be poverty traps.[46] Finally, these findings are interesting in light of those showing that respondents are much more critical of their own economic situations when they compare themselves with the rest of their country than they are when they compare themselves to those in their own communities. Safety net organizations are more likely to be within community organizations, while other kinds of organizations are more likely to provide associational ties beyond the neighborhood.

Evidence from Russia

For Russia, we have data from the Russia Longitudinal Monitoring Survey for 1995 to 1998, a period of extensive macroeconomic volatility. The RLMS interviews more than 10,000 individuals (or around 3,800 households) each year, and many are reinterviewed in the following years. When we identified

---

45. For an excellent critique of much of this literature, see Durlauf (forthcoming [a]).

46. See Hoff (1996); Durlauf (forthcoming [b]). For a description of the role of organizations such as safety nets, see Graham (1994).

the households that were also asked questions about subjective well-being and perceptions of past progress in addition to objective income data, we ended up with a panel covering more than 2,000 households.[47] Unlike in Peru, for Russia we have income rather than expenditure data, which may result in a higher degree of measurement error, particularly given the high levels of inflation during the period under study. This may explain at least part of the discrepancy that we find between perceptions and objective trends in Russia, which is markedly larger than in Peru (discussed below).

In terms of objective mobility, as in Peru, we see extensive movements both up and down the income ladder, although downward trends were more dominant in Russia. Seventy-seven percent of the population in the sample had income declines, and of these the average decline for the period was 10 percent.[48] Nearly half—48 percent—of those in the fourth quintile experienced downward mobility, with 11 percent ending up in the bottom quintile and 15 percent in the second quintile (see table 3-4). Of those who started the period in the top income quintile, only 40 percent retained their position in that quintile, while 9 percent fell to the bottom income quintile. (In Peru only 3 percent of those at the top fell to the very bottom during a much longer—nine years—period).

The results on perceptions were similar in both countries, although the negative skew was even stronger for Russia: 71 percent of those with income gains of 30 percent or more had negative assessments, and 79 percent of those with income losses accurately assessed their trajectories. In Peru, a number of respondents fared very poorly, yet assessed their situation positively, but in Russia very few assessed their situation as being better than it actually was (figure 5-4).

In Russia the frustrated achievers and their nonfrustrated counterparts had virtually identical education profiles.[49] We found that age had a quadratic effect, with the probability of being frustrated first increasing with

47. As noted earlier, the survey has been conducted in Russia since 1995 by the Russian Institute of Nutrition, University of North Carolina, and the Institute of Sociology of the Russian Academy of Sciences, with support from the World Bank, the U.S. Agency for International Development, and the National Science Foundation.

48. As in the case of Peru, we have adjusted household income for size using a 0.5 equivalence parameter.

49. For Russia we also defined frustrated achievers as those with income improvements of at least 30 percent and negative or very negative perceptions of mobility in the previous five years.

Figure 5-4. *Long-Term Perceived Mobility versus Real Income Mobility*[a]

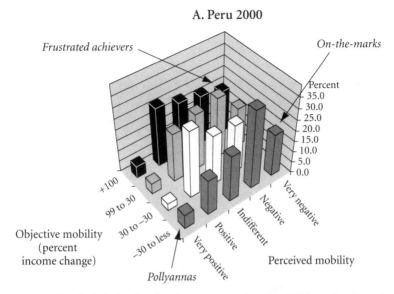

Source: Authors' calculations based on Peru survey conducted in 2000 by authors in conjunction with the Instituto Cuanto in Peru.

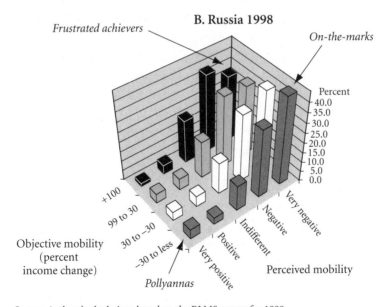

Source: Authors' calculations based on the RLMS survey for 1998.

a. Objective income mobility was measured from 1991 to 2000 for Peru and from 1995 to 1998 for Russia.

age, and then decreasing at age 54. In contrast to Peru, there were significant differences in the income trajectories of the two groups: frustrated achievers had lower mean incomes than the nonfrustrated groups; and they also experienced more income volatility (table 5-9).[50] In Peru the effects of age seem to dominate over those of income as plausible explanations for the frustrations of the achievers. In Russia both age and income matter. The frustrated achievers were, on average, more concerned about unemployment, less favorable toward the market, and less positive about democracy than the nonfrustrated group.

High levels of economic volatility in Russia affected subjective assessments. When we look at the determinants of happiness, perceived past mobility, and prospects of upward mobility, income volatility has negative effects on all three (controlling for mean income levels). In Peru, in contrast, volatility had no significant effects on any of these three variables.[51] This difference has two related plausible explanations. Volatility in Russia was slightly higher than in Peru for the periods observed.[52] And, as already noted, in Russia we relied on income, which varies more than household expenditure, which was used to measure income in Peru.

Happiness—that is, satisfaction with life—in Russia had a quadratic relationship with age, first falling until age 49 and then increasing. These findings were similar to our results for Latin America, but not for Peru. Mean happiness levels are strongly and positively correlated with income in Russia (table 5-10). Controlling for age, happiness increases with working and having been paid in the past month, but decreases for "working" in a broad sense. Being an employer has a positive effect on happiness, while being owed back wages by one's employer had the strongest negative effect on

50. They not only had a higher mean coefficient of variation, but the coefficient was significant and positive in a logit estimation with the probability of being frustrated as the dependent variable and with age, age squared, education level, and the coefficient of variation on the right side. We ran similar logit estimations for each of our perceptions variables, controlling for age, education, and income. Results are available from the authors.

51. We defined volatility as the standard deviation of household-equivalent income for the 1995–98 period and used ordered logit regressions (on economic satisfaction for Peru), and controlled for age, gender, education, and mean income levels. Results are available on request from the authors.

52. After Peru's economy was stabilized in 1990, growth rates varied considerably but the overall policy framework was far more stable than Russia's from 1995 to 1998. For our panels, meanwhile, the standard deviation in household income or expenditure for the periods observed was higher in Russia than in Peru.

Table 5-9. *Frustrated Achievers in Russia, 1998–99*

Variable	Mean			Differ- ence[a]
	Whole sample	Frustrated achievers	Non- frustrated achievers	
Age	54.47 (15.40)	51.58 (13.97)	50.37 (16.09)	...
Gender (male = 1)	0.21 (0.41)	0.24 (0.43)	0.25 (0.43)	...
Education	8.41 (2.35)	8.62 (2.13)	8.91 (1.97)	...
Equivalence household income (1998)	2,698 (2,935)	4,753 (5,964)	6,114 (5,574)	*
Coefficient of variation (1995, 1996, 1997, 1998)	0.56 (0.38)	0.64 (0.62)	0.55 (0.23)	*
Life satisfaction	1.91 (1.00)	1.82 (0.88)	2.45 (1.25)	* *
Economic ladder question	2.93 (1.48)	3.00 (1.56)	3.72 (1.52)	*
Prospect of upward mobility	2.06 (1.00)	2.07 (1.02)	2.58 (0.97)	**
Pro-democracy attitude	0.53 (0.54)	0.53 (0.45)	0.51 (0.70)	*
Satisfaction with market reform process	0.74 (0.55)	0.65 (0.59)	0.96 (0.57)	*
Fear of unemployment	3.96 (1.37)	4.15 (1.22)	3.57 (1.56)	*
Restrict the rich	3.22 (0.79)	3.16 (0.82)	2.89 (0.94)	**

Source: Authors' calculations based on RLMS Survey, 1995–98. Standard deviations are in parentheses.

a. Difference of the means between frustrated achievers and nonfrustrated achievers; * significant at the 1 percent level; ** significant at the 5 percent level.

happiness of any variable. The owner of one's place of employment (government, foreign company, and the like) has no significant effect on happiness, while concern for losing one's job has a strong negative effect. Unemployment had a strong negative effect, similar to its effect in Latin America.

RLMS respondents who said the government should not restrict the incomes of the rich were more educated, had higher incomes, and had high

Table 5-10. *Happiness in Russia, 1998*[a]

Independent variable	Coefficient
Age	−0.069
	(−3.579)
Age^2	0.001
	(3.368)
Male dummy	0.365
	(3.647)
Education	0.048
	(2.131)
Married	0.001
	(0.006)
Log income	0.498
	(9.237)
Number of observations	2,030
Pseudo R^2	(0.028)

Source: Authors' calculations based on RLMS Survey, 1995–98.
a. Ordered logit estimation. *z* statistics are in parentheses.

assessments of their future chances of getting ahead. Again, there was a quadratic relationship with age, but in this case it appeared as an inverted U, with middle-age respondents more in favor of restricting the rich than either younger or older respondents. Those in favor of such restrictions were more likely to be receiving pensions or to be employed by the government. Frustrated achievers were also more likely than nonfrustrated achievers to favor restricting the rich.

When respondents were asked whether market reforms should continue, support for the market showed a quadratic relation with age similar to the one for happiness (U-shaped, with support initially decreasing and then at a certain point increasing with age). Support for the market was higher for women than men, for those who were employed and receiving wages on time, and for those who were employed by a foreign firm. There was a negative correlation between support for the market and being employed by a Russian firm.

The economic ladder question was included in the RLMS in 1998. Average ELQ responses are slightly higher in the bottom than in the second decile and begin to increase again in the third decile (figure 5-5). A plausible explanation for this result may be the extent to which those at the low-

Figure 5-5. *Responses on Economic Ladder Question, by Decile, in Russia, 1998*

Mean response

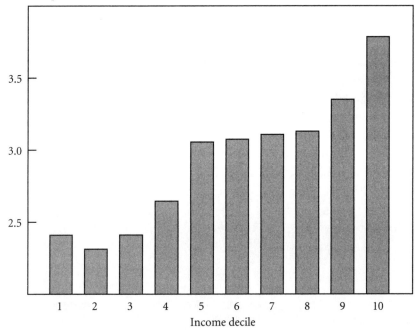

Income decile

Source: Authors' calculations, based on the RLMS survey for 1998.

est income levels are not integrated into the modern "market" economy, but instead participate in what Gaddy and Ickes call the "virtual economy," where they operate at a subsistence and barter level, working in enterprises that pay wages in kind if at all.[53] This makes it difficult to make accurate assessments about income or status.

This finding contrasts with Latin America and Peru, where average ELQ levels increase monotonically with income (see figures 5-2 and 5-3). The

53. For detail on the extent of Russia's barter and subsistence economy, see Gaddy and Ickes (1998) and Gaddy and Ickes (forthcoming). Ravallion and Loshkin also find a mismatch between actual incomes and ELQ responses. Less than half (43 percent) of the 29.4 percent of adults who placed themselves on the lowest two rungs of the ladder were also among the 32.7 percent of adults living in households with incomes below the poverty line. See Ravallion and Loshkin (1999a).

Russia sample has a higher percentage of rural respondents, and in general rural respondents tend to have lower reference norms than their urban counterparts; they are also more likely to be in the virtual economy. In Peru we found that rural respondents were less likely to place themselves on the extremes (high or low) of a perceived income ladder.[54] Finally, as in the case of happiness and assessments of past and future economic progress, income volatility (as opposed to income level) had negative and significant effects on ELQ responses in Russia. And, as in Peru, frustrated achievers had a lower mean ELQ than did their nonfrustrated counterparts.

As noted in chapter 4, the dramatic increases in poverty that occurred during the transition years in Russia generally shifted reference norms downward. Milanovic and Jovanovic find that subjective perceptions of the minimum income required for a family to live—the subjective poverty line—fell from 1993 to 1996, and by the end of the period, closely approximated the official minimum income level.[55] This latter level, initially well below the subjective level, did not increase during the period.

Conclusions

We began this chapter by suggesting that relative income differences matter more to happiness or subjective well-being than do absolute ones and that attitudes about these differences are mediated by expectations about future mobility; that respondents' positions on the income ladder matter; and that change in status—measured by income mobility—has strong effects (although not always necessarily in the expected direction).

Most studies of subjective well-being find that after a certain absolute level of basic income, relative income differences matter more than absolute ones. Our results—in particular the very negative skew in the assessments of the most upwardly mobile respondents—clearly reflect the importance of relative income differences. Upwardly mobile individuals are most likely to look beyond their original cohort for reference groups. And in very unequal societies that have adopted international consumption standards, the reference point for the upwardly mobile may seem unattainable regardless of

54. In Peru rural respondents were much less likely to opt for the extremes of any response choice.
55. Milanovic and Jovanovic (1999).

absolute income gains. The respondents in our sample tended to be much more critical when assessing their progress in comparison with their countrymen than they were relative to their community, and frustrated achievers were far more critical than the average respondent. The frustrated achievers were also more negative than the average in their assessments of their prospects for future upward mobility.

Our results also suggest that relative income differences are more important for those in the middle of the distribution than for either the very wealthy or the very poor. In the Peru sample, the most frustrated were not the poor, but those in the middle despite their absolute gains. For the Latin America sample discussed in chapter 4, the effects of wealth gains on happiness were logarithmic and were stronger for the poor than they were for those in the middle or at the top.

Income mobility also had effects on happiness, with greater objective gains often associated with increased frustration rather than increased subjective well-being. One factor here is reference groups. Another is that both the Peru and Russia surveys were conducted at times when high levels of macroeconomic volatility prevailed, with related high levels of mobility and few guarantees that income gains were either stable or permanent. We found that volatility had a clear negative effect on life satisfaction in Russia and that it increased the probability of belonging to the frustrated achiever group. Regardless of the explanation for these frustrations, all of our data suggest that frustration has negative effects on happiness.

Beyond these propositions, several additional explanations for the frustrations of our achievers are plausible. These include recall problems in assessing past earnings, particularly for nonsalaried workers, and differences among rural and urban respondents, with the latter much more willing to make extreme statements. Behavioral traits may also play a role. We know that our frustrated achievers are less happy than our nonfrustrated respondents, but we do not know the direction of causality. To answer this question, we need new data as well as the tools available to psychologists.

Our findings are preliminary ones in a research area that is fairly new, at least for the developing economies. Accepting these limitations, we believe that our results make three general contributions. First, the findings support the importance for enhancing welfare that the literature on happiness in the developed economies gives to variables other than absolute income gains. Our work highlights the role of relative differences, changes in employment and other status (uncertainty), and age, among others. Second, our analysis links the findings in the happiness literature—as well as those in our own surveys—to the broader debates on the effects of increasing international economic integration on social welfare within countries. They highlight the effects of volatility and of distributional shifts, which seem to create the most uncertainty and have the strongest effects on the attitudes of lower-middle and middle-income urban groups.

Finally, the large and consistent gap we find between objective income trends and subjective assessments of the upwardly mobile may have implications for the future economic and political behavior of precisely the group that is critical to the sustainability of market policies. As is suggested by the POUM hypothesis, public attitudes about redistribution are often mediated by individuals' expectations for future upward mobility. Our frustrated achievers had consistently lower expectations for future upward mobility.[57] The frustrated achievers in Russia, meanwhile, were more likely to support redistribution than were their nonfrustrated counterparts. More comprehensive treatment of this question—both theoretical and empirical—requires an additional stage of research.

57. The effects of current economic outcomes on future behavior, such as savings, provide a theoretical starting point for research in this area. On savings and anticipated income, see, for example, Carroll (1994). There is also some literature that uses past mobility and perceptions of future mobility to explain voting behavior and in particular attitudes toward redistribution. See Benabou and Ok (1998) and Piketty (1995). Pettinato, Hammond, and Graham (forthcoming) attempt a simple theoretical exercise to explore the potential feedback effects of the perceptions gap of our frustrated achievers. That effort uses, among other things, the methodological tools developed in Epstein and Axtell (1996).

6

Frustrated Achievers in a Global Economy: Challenges for Policy and Future Research

A central objective of this book was to suggest new ways of thinking about age-old inequality issues. We began by asking whether and how much individuals move up and down the income ladder in the context of market reforms and then explored the effects of those movements on individuals' perceived well-being. We framed our thinking around two related concepts: the differences in the way income inequality affects public attitudes, depending on its persistence (Hirschman's tunnel effect hypothesis), and how individuals' expectations about future income mobility mediate these attitudes (the POUM hypothesis).

Our findings confirmed our initial proposition that the effects of mobility on perceived well-being are moderated by relative as well as absolute income differences and by individuals' positions on the income ladder. The effects of mobility are also moderated by nonincome variables ranging from demographic traits, such as age and marital status, to macroeconomic trends, such as income volatility and inflation. We posit that trends in income mobility and individuals' perceptions of those trends may have implications for their future economic and political behavior and thus for the sustainability of market policies.

We first reported on the limited data we have on trends in mobility and opportunity in the emerging market economies. We then examined the demographic determinants of happiness or subjective well-being for the countries for which we have data—seventeen countries in Latin America and Russia—and compared them with the standard findings for the advanced industrial economies. With these findings as a baseline, we framed our analysis of the effects of mobility on perceptions around three variables that are particularly relevant in the context of emerging markets. These were the effects of market reforms on the mobility and opportunity of various age, income, and education cohorts; the manner in which respondents' real position on the income ladder mediates the effects of relative income differences on perceptions; and macroeconomic volatility and related public concerns about vulnerability and insecurity.

All of these variables indeed had effects on subjective well-being and may at least partly explain the large gap we found between individuals' objective income trajectories and their evaluations of their past progress and current economic situations. A majority of the upwardly mobile individuals in our panel samples from Peru and Russia tended to underestimate their own economic progress in their assessments of their current economic situations compared with the past and with others in their countries and communities; they were also quite pessimistic about their prospects for future mobility. These frustrated achievers tended to be in urban areas and in the middle and lower middle of the income distribution rather than at the bottom, which suggests that relative income differences and real and perceived insecurities have as much, if not more, influence than objective income trends on perceptions of well-being.

We found it both surprising and worrisome that so many individuals who are faring relatively well under market policies report deep frustration with their well-being. We explore the possible explanations for these perceptions gaps in detail, as well as their possible effects on support for market policies and for democracy, and find that the frustrated achievers are less satisfied than the nonfrustrated achievers with both market policies and democracy. (A caveat here is that we have information on attitudes about the market and democracy only for a subset of the respondents in our panel studies.) This finding contrasts with the potential virtuous circle that appears in our data for Latin America and Russia, a circle in which people who favor market policies and are satisfied with democracy are, on average, also happier.

We believe that the frustrations of these achievers merit the attention of policymakers as well as scholars, as they are driven at least in part by factors that can be influenced by policy, such as macroeconomic trends and the structure and scope of social policy.

Mobility Trends

Our discussion of mobility in chapter 3 showed how two societies with identical distributions, as measured by traditional yardsticks such as the Gini, can be very different if fairness is gauged by equality of opportunity. A completely immobile society, where there is no room for advancement, would obviously be unacceptable to most people. Yet a society with complete mobility, where parents were not able to pass on genetic endowments or to make investments in their children's education, would also not be acceptable to the average respondent.

In most advanced economies the rate and degree of income mobility is moderated by gradual structural changes in the larger economy and by public policies in a host of areas, particularly education. In most developing economies these same factors are at play, but policy reforms and rapid integration into the world economy, together with related changes in the structure and scope of public expenditures, have resulted in much more dramatic structural changes, with consequent effects on mobility.

The available data on mobility trends show a remarkable amount of movement up and down the income ladder in the developing economies in comparison with advanced industrial ones. In those countries where reforms have been fully implemented, the turn to the market seems to have eliminated many distortions that blocked the productive potential and upward mobility of the poor. Yet at the same time the turn to the market has created new insecurities and new vulnerabilities, particularly for those in the middle of the income distribution without high level skills or education.

In periods as short as three years, individuals have moved up two or even three income deciles, but others who were previously in the middle strata are falling into poverty. Individuals (usually young) with skills and education have for the most part fared exceptionally well. Trade integration and technology- and skill-driven growth have dramatically increased the marginal returns to higher education relative to lower levels, and the margin of reward between secondary and primary education has narrowed considerably. For Latin America in the 1990s, rewards to workers with higher education are large relative to workers with both primary and secondary levels.

Two related phenomena are relevant to our analysis here.[1] These are top-driven inequality and middle-income stress. Both result in part from education trends and at the same time deepen the impact of these trends on public perceptions. Inequality driven by concentration of wealth at the top of the distribution is particularly prevalent in Latin America and highlights the issue of relative income differences. Much of the inequality in Latin America recorded by the Gini coefficient is driven by differences between those in the top half of the top decile and the rest of the distribution. This top-driven inequality, coupled with more insecurity for those in the middle, results in a middle-class squeeze or "stress" of sorts. We measure this stress as the distance between the median income and that of the group that produces the top 50 percent of national income. In many countries, particularly those that have implemented market reforms in an incomplete manner, this distance is large and growing. Not surprisingly, we find that these trends in mobility and inequality have effects on individuals' subjective well-being in the emerging market economies.

Happiness, Markets, and Democracy in New Market Economies

To date little of the literature on happiness or subjective well-being has focused on developing economies.[2] Our exploration of the available data for Latin America and Russia found that the demographic determinants of happiness in these places are remarkably similar to those in the advanced industrial economies. It is particularly notable that the findings are consistent across seventeen Latin American countries with different levels of per capita income and with different policy regimes. Our findings suggest—as do most of the studies of happiness for the advanced economies—that there are strong, behaviorally driven determinants of utility that may be worthy of more attention than they typically receive in traditional economic models.

In Latin America and Russia, as in the developed economies, the age effects on happiness are clear, with the age coefficient having a quadratic

---

1. Birdsall, Graham, and Pettinato (2000).
2. We review the literature on happiness in developed economies in detail in chapter 2.

effect. In Latin America happiness first declines with age and then increases, beginning at about age 47, a curve very similar to those of the developed economies. Age has a similar quadratic effect in Russia, although the turning point is later, at age 62 (obviously, then, not many people in Russia actually live to experience the upward part of the curve, and one might assume that in general happiness is downward sloping with age there). Wealthier people are, on average, happier than poor people in both Latin America and Russia, as they are in the advanced economies. Education is also positively correlated with happiness in both contexts, although the coefficient is usually rendered insignificant when income is included in the equation, as the effects run in the same direction and those of income are predominant.[3]

One difference is gender. In the United States women tend to be happier than men, while in Latin America there are no significant differences between the genders. In contrast, men in Russia are happier than women. A plausible, although far from definitive, explanation is that women in Russia may still face more discrimination than they do in the other economies.

In all three places, being unemployed has significant and negative effects on happiness. One difference is that being self-employed is positively correlated with happiness in the developed economies, yet negatively correlated in the developing ones. In the United States being self-employed is usually a choice reflecting more freedom in one's employment situation, whereas in Latin America and Russia, most self-employed people have a precarious existence in the informal sector. Retirement, meanwhile, has no effects on happiness in either Latin America or the United States. In Russia, however, being retired is negatively correlated with happiness. Given the well-known plight of pensioners in Russia, this is no surprise.

In the developed economies, both inflation and the rate of unemployment have significant and negative effects on happiness, with the effects of inflation having slightly more weight.[4] In Latin America, inflation has negative effects on happiness, but the rate of unemployment is insignificant. *Fear* of unemployment, which has significant and negative effects on happiness in both Latin America and Russia, seems a more relevant variable than the rate of unemployment in economies where the formal unemployment

---

3. The coefficient remains significant for Russia but not for the larger Latin America sample.

4. Di Tella, MacCulloch, and Oswald (1997).

rate disguises the prevalence of insecure informal sector jobs and the absence of adequate unemployment insurance.

We could not find any discernible evidence of the general effects of market reforms on happiness. Among other things, evaluating countries' reform progress is extremely difficult and fraught with time inconsistency problems. A pro-market attitude was positively correlated with happiness in both Latin America and Russia. Individual satisfaction with democracy had an additional and positive effect on happiness in Latin America. In Russia, not wanting to return to socialism—a very weak proxy for democratic attitudes—had a positive effect on happiness. As cautious optimists we suggest that there may be a virtuous circle, in which pro-market attitudes, satisfaction with democracy, and life satisfaction reinforce each other.

The potential of such a virtuous circle to reinforce democracy and sustain markets, however, depends on its overall size and its applicability to a wide majority of the population. Positive rankings on both the preference for democracy variable and the index of support for market policies are strongly linked to income or wealth levels (or both). In addition, we found a very strong negative skew on the perceptions of past mobility of those in the lower middle of the distribution.

Several theoretical and empirical studies find that past mobility experiences can result in persistent political attitudes. Thus, one way to strengthen political support in developing economies for both democracy and markets may be to introduce policies that enhance mobility for those on the middle and lower rungs of the income ladder and that generate a more widely held belief that upward mobility is a probability rather than a remote possibility. In other words, if mobility experiences have an impact on political attitudes, and happier people with a positive view of their prospects for upward mobility are also more supportive of democracy and market policies, one way to expand this virtuous circle is to facilitate upward mobility for a wider range of people.

Mobility Trends and Perceptions Gaps

In chapter 5 we looked more closely at the effects of mobility trends on individuals' perceptions of well-being and on their views of their status relative to others in their reference groups. Most studies of subjective well-being find that, above a certain absolute level of basic income, relative income differences influence perceptions of well-being more than absolute ones do. For the Latin America sample, the effects of wealth gains on happiness were logarithmic and were stronger for the poor than they were for those in the middle or at the top.

The results of the Peru and Russia surveys results also clearly highlight the importance of relative income differences. Particularly notable was the very negative skew in the subjective assessments of the most upwardly mobile respondents. These are the individuals that are most likely to look beyond their original cohort for reference groups. And in very unequal societies that have adopted international consumption standards, the reference point for the upwardly mobile may seem unattainable regardless of absolute income gains. The respondents in our sample tended to be much more critical when assessing their progress compared with that of their country than they were compared with their community, and frustrated achievers were far more critical than the average respondent. They were also less positive about their prospects for future upward mobility. Our results also suggest that relative income differences are more important for those in the middle of the distribution than for either the very wealthy or the very poor. In the Peru sample, those in the middle, not the poor, were the most frustrated despite their absolute gains.

Income mobility also has effects on "happiness," with greater objective gains more often associated with increased frustration than with increased subjective well-being. One factor explaining this phenomenon is reference groups. Another factor is that the Peru and Russia surveys were conducted at times of high levels of macroeconomic volatility, with related high levels of mobility and very few guarantees that income gains would be stable or permanent. Volatility had a clear negative effect on life satisfaction in Russia, and it increased the probability of being a frustrated achiever.

Several additional factors may help account for the high level of frustrated achievers in our samples. These include recall problems in assessing past earnings, particularly for nonsalaried workers, and differences among rural and urban respondents, with the latter much more willing to make extreme statements. In Peru the frustrated achievers were significantly older than the nonfrustrated achievers. Behavioral traits may also play a role: we know that the frustrated achievers are not as "happy" as nonfrustrated respondents, but we do not know the direction of causality. To answer this question, we need new data as well as the tools available to psychologists.

Regardless of the reasons for these frustrations, we find it somewhat worrisome that so many individuals who are faring relatively well economically evaluate their well-being or economic status negatively and also have lower than average expectations for their future prospects. Many of them are also less satisfied with both democracy and markets. Some of the explanation is behavioral and beyond the influence of policy. Yet part of it lies in macroeconomic volatility and in the structure of labor markets and social insurance systems in these countries, all of which can be influenced by public policy.[5]

Implications for Policy and Research

The findings reported here are preliminary in a research area that is fairly new, at least for the developing economies. Accepting these limitations, we believe that our results make three general contributions. First, they support the findings in the literature on happiness in the developed economies, which emphasize the importance of variables other than absolute income gains in enhancing welfare: relative differences, changes in employment and other status (uncertainty), and age, among others.

Second, our analysis links the findings in the happiness literature—as well as those in our own surveys—to the broader debates on the effects of increasing international economic integration on social welfare within countries. Our results highlight the effects of volatility and distributional shifts, which appear to have stronger effects on the attitudes of lower- and middle-income urban groups than on those of the very poor or the wealthy.

Moreover, the large and consistent gap we find between objective income trends and subjective assessments of the upwardly mobile may have implications for the future economic and political behavior of a group that is critical to the sustainability of market policies.[6] We are by no means sug-

5. As noted in chapter 5, we ideally would like to gauge the balance of the effects that are behaviorally driven versus those that are not, but we are at this point unable to include person fixed effects in our regressions; as a result of the expansion of the Peru panel in the year 2000, we do not have matching perceptions data for each of the three years (1991, 1994, and 1996) for the full 500-person panel.

6. The effects of current economic outcomes on future behavior, such as savings, provide a theoretical starting point for research in this area, as is discussed in detail in chapter 5. Some literature uses past mobility and perceptions of future mobility to explain voting behavior and

gesting that attention should be diverted from the need for poverty reduction. But the debate on the effects of globalization should focus some attention on the fate and attitudes of the near poor as well as the poor. Although we do not yet know whether or how these attitudes translate into actual behavior, we believe that the negative skews that we find are stark and consistent enough to merit additional attention.

Third, our research establishes links between positive evaluations of well-being and support for democracy and market policies. Individuals with higher levels of income tend to evaluate their well-being in a more positive manner. The POUM hypothesis posits that those with higher expectations for future progress are less likely to support high levels of redistributive taxation. The frustrated achievers, who have lower expectations for future progress, tend to be more supportive of redistribution. Thus paying attention to the frustrations of our less wealthy achievers might be one way to contribute to support for markets and democracy. To repeat, this does not mean that resources should be diverted from the poorest, but that new attention should be paid to the plight of those in the middle strata, who are often near poor. Without the political support of this group, it may be very difficult to sustain and deepen the policy reforms that most developing countries have implemented in the past decade. A reversal of these policies would have very high economic costs, costs that the poor can least afford to absorb.

Policies to Enhance Opportunity and Reduce Insecurity

Three sets of policies could reduce the insecurity and enhance the upward mobility of both the middle strata and the poor. The first of these would make social services more broadly available. The key component here is education policies that make obtaining jobs in high-technology, high-skill economic sectors a more attainable objective for a broader section of society. The second set of policies would remove distortions in markets and public policies that block the productive potential of low-income groups. One key distortion is excessive levels of inequality. The third set of policies would provide a better safety net and other forms of unemployment insurance.

---

in particular attitudes toward redistribution; see Benabou and Ok (1998) and Piketty (1995). Pettinato, Hammond, and Graham (forthcoming) attempt a simple theoretical exercise to explore the potential feedback effects of this perceptions gap.

BROADENING SOCIAL SERVICES. The first and most obvious way of enhancing the mobility and opportunity of both the poor and those in the middle-income strata is improving access to good-quality education beyond the secondary level, including vocational and technical education. Although the long-term benefits of such a policy shift are evident, sustained political commitment, institutional development, and substantial resources will be necessary to implement and maintain a policy change that will not yield results for several years.

Fundamental to delivering more and higher-quality education is a more comprehensive social contract for delivering essential social services in general. Policymakers and others are currently engaged in debate about the merits of targeting welfare to specific groups. Some argue, for example, that tightly targeted policies cannot sustain the political support necessary to preserve their public funding and that the better option is to make social welfare programs available to a broader segment of society.[7]

In several developing countries, however, increased targeting of public social expenditures, supported by changes in welfare policies, has effectively reduced absolute poverty, particularly during periods of fiscal austerity.[8] At the same time, globalization-related shifts in the rewards to different education and skill cohorts, coupled with a shrinking of the size and scope of public services, have substantially lowered the social insurance available to those in the lower middle and middle of the income distribution. This insecurity may be one factor contributing to the frustrations of the achievers.

Without reversing any achievements on the poverty reduction front, it may be necessary to reexamine targeting policies. At least some targeting is still desirable in most developing economies, where public resources are limited and great effort has been made to establish fiscal stability. Accepting these constraints, the discussion about targeting policy should move toward crafting a broader and more politically sustainable social contract that

7. See, for example, the debate on targeted versus universal services between Greenstein (1991) and Skocpol (1991). For a more theoretical exploration of this topic, see Pritchett and Gelbard (1997).

8. A classic example is the case of Chile in the 1980s and early 1990s. For detail, see the chapters on Chile in Graham (1994) and Graham (1998). Another example is the case of Peru; see Graham and Kane (1998).

includes middle-income groups as well as the poor. The nature and extent of that contract will, of course, take time to work out and will vary across countries, as will the role played by the private sector.[9]

In addition to supply-side policies, the demand side may also have to be addressed. A wide body of literature traces the ways persistent social norms, identity, and low expectations perpetuate patterns of inequality.[10] Some societies, where the poor have no tradition of higher-level education, may need policies to educate and encourage low-income people to make new kinds of investments in their children's future.[11] A set of education policies that does not address both demand and supply sides is unlikely to break the strong intergenerational determinants of educational achievement, which is necessary to enhance mobility over the long term.

REDUCING DISTORTIONS. The second set of policies must address existing distortions in markets and failures in government policies. Many countries in the developing world, particularly in Latin America, have made major strides in improving their macroeconomic frameworks and reducing such distortions. Significantly, in those countries in Latin America that have implemented coherent reforms (and for which we have data), the middle class is growing, rather than shrinking.[12]

Yet, as in the case of improving education systems, removing distortions alone is not enough. If poorly performing public monopolies are merely replaced with poorly performing private ones, as has occurred in some countries, the outcome is likely to be persistent, or even increased, inequality and few, if any, new opportunities for the poor or near poor. Given that the removal of distortions and the opening to free trade is clearly rewarding the most educated groups the most—at least for Latin America, where we have the most recent evidence—there is much margin for improving the

9. For a review of several experiments with varying degrees of private sector involvement in this area, see Graham (1998).

10. See, for example, Durlauf (1996); Young (1994); Akerlof (1997).

11. Previous research on reforms to social service provision, such as vouchers in education and local management boards in education, for example, suggests that the poorest tend to be the least likely to participate, due to marginal but preclusive transaction costs, the high opportunity costs of their time, and low expectations; see Graham (1998).

12. It is quite plausible that there are some important exceptions to the relationship between improved macroeconomic frameworks and the size of the middle class, for which we do not have data, such as India and China.

education and skills of the poor so that they can take advantage of new opportunities that arise.[13] As in the case of education, supply-side and demand-side policies must reinforce each other.

Addressing the issue of inequality must be part of the policy package reducing distortions. The high costs to economic growth of excessive concentration of income and assets have been well-documented elsewhere.[14] Hirschman's tunnel hypothesis suggests that persistent inequality—in contrast to initial changes in the distribution—can lead to broader public frustration. Our results suggest that high levels of inequality, particularly top-driven inequality, have additional costs in that they create an unachievable reference bar that frustrates even the most upwardly mobile individuals. These frustrations, in turn, may well have effects on political support for the kinds of market-enhancing policies that can deliver sustained growth and poverty reduction. The POUM hypothesis, for example, posits that individuals with higher prospects of upward mobility are less likely to provide political support for high levels of redistribution.

We believe that a more broadly held perception, as well as a reality, of enhanced equality of opportunity and a more level playing field should result in increased and more sustainable political support for market policies and integration in the global economy. Moreover, if the poor perceive that the playing field is level and that opportunities do indeed exist, they will be much more likely to invest in their children's education and therefore their ability to take up those opportunities in the future.

PROVIDING ADEQUATE SAFETY NETS. A third set of policies, one that is essential both to enhancing opportunities and to ensuring awareness of the existence of those opportunities, is the provision of adequate safety nets not only for those who take risks to get ahead and run into trouble, but also for those who fall behind because they are unable to take up new opportunities. The absence of adequate insurance mechanisms and safety nets can themselves result in market distortions, as those who are employed seek to minimize risk and guarantee employment security through whatever mechanisms are available, even though they may be extremely inefficient (such as excessively rigid labor laws). In addition, the insecurity caused by weak

13. The data for Latin America are from Behrman, Birdsall, and Székely (2000a) and are discussed in greater detail in chapter 3.

14. See, for example, Birdsall and Londoño (1997); Birdsall, Pinckney, and Sabot (1999); and Birdsall, Ross, and Sabot (1995).

insurance mechanisms in the face of exogenously driven volatility and constantly changing rewards to labor sectors is, no doubt, one of the factors that drives the negative skew on the perceptions of frustrated achievers.

Two kinds of safety nets are necessary. One is concerned with unemployment insurance and other forms of social insurance, which allow workers to risk taking up new opportunities by protecting them from unexpected income shocks caused by macroeconomic volatility and other exogenous shocks. The second kind of safety net addresses the needs of the poorest who fall behind, either because of low skills or because of health and other shocks that prevent them from participating even in the low-skilled sector of the economy. Safety nets have received a fair amount of the attention in the past but usually in the context of fiscal adjustments. We argue that policymakers need to develop more permanent safety nets that can expand and contract as needed, providing a buffer during cyclical fluctuations or downturns caused by externally driven exogenous shocks.[15]

Implications for Future Research

Our findings raise several questions and issues directly relevant to policy, but they also pose several questions that require further research. Although these questions are not directly linked to policy, in the end finding answers to them is essential to informing future policy. The kinds of policies that we are suggesting here cannot be accurately designed without adequate data about mobility and its links to the global economy and without knowing the effects of those trends on the perceived well-being of the individuals whose welfare the policies seek to enhance. First, more—and more complete—data are needed on mobility trends, rates, and their determinants, particularly for the developing economies. The fast-paced nature of change in the global economy and of technology-driven growth mandates a more dynamic view of poverty reduction based on a better understanding of income mobility and related movements in and out of poverty.

Second, the wide discrepancies between objective mobility trends and individuals' assessments of those trends suggest that more—and more complete—data are needed on public perceptions. Two kinds of data are necessary.

---

15. For past discussion of this issue, see Graham (1994). Lustig (2001), meanwhile, is one of the few authors that has consistently stressed the need for more permanent and institutionalized safety net mechanisms.

The first is more survey data on perceptions. One example is the Latinobarometro survey, which includes questions about life satisfaction and individual assessments of their economic situations compared with the past and with others in a variety of reference groups. The Latinobarometro also covers attitudes about market policies and democracy, which allows us to identify at least some correlations between subjective well-being and political preferences. Efforts are currently under way to launch similar surveys in several regions, including Africa, Asia, and Eastern Europe, which would substantially broaden the available database. Financing these surveys is difficult, however, and is usually done through private subscriptions, which limits the availability of the data for independent researchers. Support from the international financial institutions, as well as from academic institutions interested in using the data, could help guarantee broader public access.

The one limitation of these regional surveys, however, is that they do not usually provide panel data. Panel data surveys are more complicated and expensive to administer but have clear advantages because the same individuals are followed over time. One of our own future objectives is to improve and repeat the Peru perceptions survey, which is part of a panel, and to administer it in several other countries in Latin America. The Russian RLMS, some of which is also panel data, is scheduled for at least one more repetition. Continuing it would provide a valuable resource for future research. We hope that the current interest in the effects of globalization on poverty and inequality worldwide will spawn a broader effort—most likely in the international financial institutions—to establish permanent panel studies in developing economies similar to those in the United States and other advanced economies.

The second kind of data needed are more novel and will entail the collaboration of psychologists and social scientists. One important and unresolved issue in this book is the extent to which the frustrations that we find are driven by behavior. In other words, a certain percentage of each population may be frustrated regardless of objective economic conditions. Along the same vein, the survey data link the effects of democracy, market reforms, and macroeconomic trends to happiness, but they do not establish the direction of causality. It may well be that happy people are satisfied no matter what policy regime they live under.

It is possible that causality may run in both directions. We nonetheless believe that nonbehavioral variables, such as income mobility, macroeconomic volatility, and occupational status, have an additional influence on perceptions. These are clearly areas where policy has a great deal of room to influence outcomes. Understanding the balance between behavioral and exogenous effects on perceptions of economic progress and status, however, is essential to designing appropriate policies.

Progress in this arena will require more of the nascent collaboration between economists and psychologists that characterizes the growing field of behavioral economics and the related research on happiness and subjective well-being.[16] Progress will also entail applying such an approach to the issues particular to the developing economies. Further research in this area could contribute to two questions that have important implications for policy.

The first question concerns the definition of utility or welfare. Economists and psychologists debate the roles of preferences (which are assumed to be rationally determined) and attitudes in explaining economic behavior. Recent work by psychologist Daniel Kahneman and colleagues suggests that attitudes predominate when individuals make hypothetical decisions, such as when they attach a dollar value to a public good or to a future acquisition, while the rational decisionmaking model is more applicable to consequential decisions.[17] Yet the range of decisions covered by each of these categories is not clear cut, and overlap is often substantial.[18]

Most standard economic models are based on the rational decisionmaking model and on revealed preferences rather than attitudes, in part because economists have traditionally been skeptical of the merit and reliability of

16. Early work in this arena was pioneered by economists such as George Akerlof and Richard Thaler, and psychologists such as Daniel Kahneman and Amos Tversky. See, for example, Akerlof and Kranton (2000); Kahneman and Tversky (2000); and Kahneman, Diener, and Schwarz (1999).

17. The authors also make the point that these valuations are susceptible to framing effects, inadequately sensitive to scope, and severely context dependent; see Kahneman, Ritov, and Schkade (1999). Yet if sufficient care is taken to account for these problems, the affective value that people attach to issues conveys useful information about their possible reactions to policy proposals or to actual outcomes. We are grateful to Henry Aaron for suggesting this reference.

18. Decisions about future savings and investments, for example, could fall under both categories, particularly if one considers that many individuals—particularly those with low education—make such decisions with little basis for predicting future earnings.

data on subjective well-being. In contrast, psychologists have worked with such data for years and have provided evidence of what they describe as "validation." In recent years, however, an increasing number of economists have begun to use the data on attitudes (even though recognizing their limitations) to delve into questions for which income-based criteria alone provide insufficient explanation.[19] Recent work by Keely, for example, explores theoretically how utilizing psychologists' concept of hedonic adaptation—a process by which the cognitive effects of a repeated experience, such as consumption, are reduced—would change standard assumptions about utility. In particular she explores the potential effects on income and consumption, positing that hedonic adaptation may not represent a link between the absolute change in income and well-being, but rather the rate of change relative to the starting level of income. Her theoretical application is remarkably close to our empirical findings of the logarithmic effects of income mobility—rather than income levels—on reported well-being.[20]

Along the same vein, very few economic models take into account concern for relative income differences or expectations about future prospects for upward mobility. Yet the issue of relative income differences—and of how future mobility might narrow those differences—may be better fitted by an attitude-based model of decisionmaking than one based on rational decisionmaking. Our surveys show attitudes about relative differences vary greatly depending on demographic variables such as age and on the respondent's position on the income ladder. The research and the tools of social psychologists and sociologists are also relevant to exploring this issue.

An important question is whether the effects we found in this preliminary work are as consistent as our work suggests and whether they will hold over longer periods of time and in a larger sample of countries. If they do, then they could have implications for the assumptions underlying the definition of utility under certain circumstances. Assumptions about projected savings behavior or about responses to marginal tax rates, for example, are critical to policy design and outcomes.

19. In addition to the several works we have already cited, see the year 2000 issues of the *Journal of Happiness Studies*, a joint effort launched by economists and psychologists. For an economist's view on the debate of environment versus genetics in determining behavior, see Dickens and Flynn (2001).

20. Keely (2001).

Revised assumptions about utility could also have implications for both design and outcomes of a range of other policies, such as social welfare, social security, and other forms of social insurance. Attitude-based data have limitations, to be sure, but an approach that takes concerns about relative income differences more fully into account could benefit analyses in these areas.

Further research could also illuminate the possible feedback effects of gaps between perceptions and reality in evaluating economic progress. Do the frustrations of achievers lead them to work harder to earn more income and to invest in their children's education so that they get further ahead? Or does their frustration instead encourage achievers to spend conspicuously to keep up with the Jones?[21] These perceptions gaps could affect political behavior as well. Are frustrated achievers more likely to support redistribution because they have lower expectations about their future progress? Do the frustrations of the achievers in Russia, who report less satisfaction with both markets and democracy, mean that they vote for politicians who oppose the system? Will such frustrations drive the backlash against reform and globalization that so many observers warn is on the way?

At this point these questions can only be answered theoretically.[22] The research efforts necessary to answer them empirically require new ways of thinking about old problems, new data, new kinds of data, and new methods that challenge established assumptions and merge disciplines traditionally operated quite separately from one another. We hope that such efforts will inform policymakers in a globally integrated economy in the future as well as contribute to social science research more generally.

21. The possible channels for each of these outcomes are discussed in detail in chapter 2.

22. Pettinato, Hammond, and Graham (forthcoming) attempt a simple exercise of this kind in a forthcoming paper, in which we incorporate relative differences into our concept of utility, and then explore the possible feedback effects that frustrations about relative income differences can have on future economic behavior.

References

Akerlof, George. 1997. "Social Distance and Social Decisions." *Econometrica* 65 (September): 1005–27.

Akerlof, George, and Rachel Kranton. 2000. "Economics and Identity." *Quarterly Journal of Economics* 115 (August): 715–54.

Alesina, Alberto, Rafael Di Tella, and Robert MacCulloch. 2000. "Inequality and Happiness: Are Europeans and Americans Different?" Harvard University and London School of Economics (December).

Alesina, Alberto, and Roberto Perotti. 1994. "The Political Economy of Growth: A Critical Review of the Recent Literature." *World Bank Economic Review* 8(3): 351–72.

Argyle, Michael. 1999. "Causes and Correlates of Happiness." In Kahneman, Diener, and Schwarz (1999), 353–73.

Axelrod, Robert. 1984. *The Evolution of Cooperation*. Basic Books.

Barro, Robert. 1999. "Inequality, Growth, and Investment." Working Paper 7038. Cambridge, Mass.: National Bureau of Economic Research (March).

Baulch, Bob, and John Hoddinott. 2000. "Economic Mobility and Poverty Dynamics in Developing Countries." *Journal of Development Studies* 36 (August): 1–24.

Behrman, Jere. 2000. "Social Mobility: Concepts and Measurement Issues in Latin America and the Caribbean." In Birdsall and Graham (2000), 69–100.

Behrman, Jere R., Nancy Birdsall, and Miguel Székely. 2000a. "Economic Reform and Wage Differentials in Latin America." Working Paper 435. Washington: Inter-American Development Bank (October).

———. 2000b. "Intergenerational Mobility in Latin America: Deeper Markets and Better Schools Make a Difference." In Birdsall and Graham (2000), 135–67.

Benabou, Roland, and Efe Ok. 1998. "Social Mobility and the Demand for Redistribution: The POUM Hypothesis." Working Paper 6795. Cambridge, Mass.: National Bureau of Economic Research.

Berry, Albert. 1996. "The Income Distribution Threat in Latin America." *Latin American Research Review* 32 (2): 3–40.

Bertrand, Marianne, and Sendhil Mullainathan. 2001. "Do People Mean What They Say? Implications for Subjective Survey Data." Cambridge, Mass.: National Bureau of Economic Research.

Birdsall, Nancy, and Carol Graham, eds. 2000. *New Markets, New Opportunities? Economic and Social Mobility in a Changing World*. Brookings and Carnegie Endowment for International Peace.

Birdsall, Nancy, Carol Graham, and Stefano Pettinato. 2000. "Stuck in the Tunnel: Have New Markets Muddled the Middle?" Working Paper 14. Brookings, Center on Social and Economic Dynamics (August).

Birdsall, Nancy, Carol Graham, and Richard Sabot, eds. 1998. *Beyond Tradeoffs: Market Reforms and Equitable Growth in Latin America*. Brookings and the Inter-American Development Bank.

Birdsall, Nancy, and Juan Luis Londoño. 1997. "Asset Inequality Matters: An Assessment of the World Bank's Approach to Poverty Reduction." *American Economic Review* 87 (May, *Papers and Proceedings*): 32–7.

Birdsall, Nancy, Thomas Pinckney, and Richard Sabot. 1999. "Equity, Savings, and Growth." Working Paper 18. Brookings, Center on Social and Economic Dynamics (October).

Birdsall, Nancy, David Ross, and Richard Sabot. 1995. "Inequality and Growth Reconsidered." *World Bank Economic Review* 9 (September): 477–503.

Blanchflower, David G., and Andrew J. Oswald. 1999. "Well-Being over Time in Britain and the USA." Warwick University (November).

Bruno, Michael, Martin Ravallion, and Lyn Squire. 1996. "Equity and Growth in Developing Countries: Old and New Perspectives on the Policy Issues." Policy Research Working Paper 1563. Washington: World Bank (January).

Burtless, Gary. 1999. "Effects of Growing Wage Disparities and Changing Family Composition on the U.S. Income Distribution." Working Paper 4. Brookings, Center on Social and Economic Dynamics (July).

Carothers, Thomas. 1999. *Aiding Democracy Abroad: The Learning Curve*. Washington: Carnegie Endowment for International Peace.

Carroll, Christopher D. 1994. "How Does Future Income Affect Current Consumption?" *Quarterly Journal of Economics* 109 (February): 111–47.

Carter, Michael, and Julian May. 1999. "One Kind of Freedom: Poverty Dynamics in Post-Apartheid South Africa." University of Wisconsin, Department of Agricultural and Applied Economics (December).

Clark, Andrew E., and Andrew J. Oswald. 1996. "Satisfaction and Comparison of Income." *Journal of Public Economics* 61 (3): 359–81.

Clifford, P., and A. F. Heath. 1993. "The Political Consequences of Social Mobility." *Journal of the Royal Statistical Society* 156 (1): 51–61.

Cole, Harold L., George J. Mailath, and Andrew Postlewaite. 1995. "Incorporating Concern for Relative Wealth into Economic Models." *Federal Reserve Bank of Minneapolis Quarterly Review* 19 (Summer): 12–21.

Collier, Paul. 1998. "Social Capital and Poverty." Social Capital Initiative Working Paper 4. Washington: World Bank, Social Capital Initiative (December).

Conlisk, John. 1996. "Why Bounded Rationality?" *Journal of Economic Literature* 34 (June): 669–700.

Cowan, K., and José de Gregorio. 2000. "Distribution and Poverty in Chile Today: Have We Gained Ground?" In *Distributive Justice and Economic Development. The Case of Chile and Developing Countries,* edited by Andrés Solimano, Eduardo Aninat, and Nancy Birdsall. University of Michigan Press.

Cuánto, S. A. 1999. "Percepción de la Movilidad Social en el Perú, 1999." Lima, Peru.

Dahan, Momi, and Alejandro Gaviria. 1999. "Sibling Correlations and Social Mobility in Latin America." Washington: Inter-American Development Bank, Office of the Chief Economist (February).

Davis, Steven J. 1992. "Cross-Country Patterns of Change in Relative Wages." *NBER Macroeconomics Annual,* 239–92. Cambridge, Mass.: National Bureau of Economic Research.

Deaton, Angus, and Christina Paxson. 1994. "Intertemporal Choice and Inequality." *Journal of Political Economy* 102 (3): 437–67.

De Ferranti, David, and others. 2000. *Securing Our Future in a Global Economy.* Washington: World Bank.

de Tocqueville, Alexis. 1969. *Democracy in America.* Edited by J. P. Mayer. Anchor Books.

Dickens, William T., and James R. Flynn. 2001. "Heritability Estimates versus Large Environmental Effects: The IQ Paradox Resolved." *Psychological Review* 108 (2): 346–69.

Diener, Ed. 1984. "Subjective Well-Being." *Psychological Bulletin* 95 (3): 542–75.

Diener, Ed, and Eunkook Mark Suh. 1999. "National Differences in Subjective Well-Being." In Kahneman, Diener, and Schwartz (1999).

Diener, Ed, and Robert Biswas-Diener. 1999. "Income and Subjective Well-Being: Will Money Make Us Happy?" University of Illinois, Department of Psychology (December).

Diener, Ed, and others. 1993. "The Relationship between Income and Subjective Well-Being: Relative or Absolute?" *Social Indicators Research* 28: 195–223.

Dietz, Henry. 1998. *Urban Poverty, Political Participation, and the State: Lima 1970–1990.* University of Pittsburgh Press.

Di Tella, Rafael, Robert J. MacCulloch, and Andrew J. Oswald. 1997. "The Macroeconomics of Happiness." Discussion Paper Series 19. Oxford University, Centre for Economic Performance.

Dollar, David, and Aart Kray. 2000. "Growth Is Good for the Poor." Washington: World Bank, Development Research Group.

Dominitz, Jeff, and Charles Manski. 1996. "Perceptions of Economic Insecurity: Evidence from The Survey of Economic Expectations." Working Paper 5690. Cambridge, Mass.: National Bureau of Economic Research (July).

Duesenberry, James S. 1949. *Income, Saving, and the Theory of Consumer Behavior.* Harvard University Press.

Duncan, Greg, Timothy Smeeding, and Willard Rogers. 1993. "W(h)ither the Middle Class? A Dynamic View." In *Poverty and Prosperity in the United States in the Late 20th Century,* edited by Dimitri Papadimitriou and Edward Wolff. Macmillian.

Durlauf, Steven. 1996. "A Theory of Persistent Income Inequality." *Journal of Economic Growth* 1 (1): 75–94.

———. Forthcoming (a). "Bowling Alone: A Review Essay." *Journal of Economic Behavior and Organization.*

———. Forthcoming (b). "Neighborhood Feedback Effects, Endogenous Stratification, and Income Inequality." In *Disequilibrium Dynamics: Theory and Applications,* edited by William Barnett, Giancarlo Gandolfo, and Claud Hillinger. Cambridge University Press.

Duryea, Suzanne, and Miguel Székely. 1998. "Labor Markets in Latin America: A Supply Side Story." OCE Working Paper 374. Washington: Inter-American Development Bank (September).

Easterlin, Richard A. 1974. "Does Economic Growth Improve the Human Lot? Some Empirical Evidence." In *Nations and Households in Economic Growth,* edited by Paul A. David and Melvin W. Reder. New York: Academic Press.

———. 1995. "Will Raising the Incomes of All Increase the Happiness of All?" *Journal of Economic Behavior and Organization* 27 (June): 35–48.

———. 2000. "Where is Economic Growth Taking Us?" Paper presented at Mount Holyoke Conference on "The World Economy in the 21st Century: Challenges and Opportunities." South Hadley, Mass. (February 18–19).

———. 2001. "Life Cycle Welfare: Trends and Differences." *Journal of Happiness Studies,* Vol. 2, pp. 1–12.

ECLAC (Economic Commission for Latin America and the Caribbean). 2000. *The Equity Gap: A Second Assessment.* Santiago.

Epstein, Joshua, and Robert Axtell. 1996. *Growing Artificial Societies.* Brookings.

Erikson, Robert, and John H. Goldthorpe. 1985. "Are American Rates of Social Mobility Exceptionally High? New Evidence on an Old Issue." *European Sociological Review* 1 (1): 1–22.

Esping-Andersen, Gosta. 1990. *Three Worlds of Welfare Capitalism.* Princeton University Press.

Evans, Geoffrey, and Stephen Whitefield. 1995. "The Politics and Economics of Democratic Commitment: Support for Democracy in Transition Societies." *Journal of Political Science* 25: 485–514.

Fields, Gary. 2000. "Income Mobility: Concepts and Measures." In Birdsall and Graham (2000), 101–34.

Fields, Gary, and Efe Ok. 1999. "The Measurement of Income Mobility: An Introduction to the Literature." In *Handbook of Income Inequality Measurement*, edited by Jacques Silber. Kluwer Academic Publishing.

Figini, Paolo. 1998. "Inequality Measures, Equivalence Scales, and Adjustment for Household Size and Composition." Working Paper 185. Luxembourg: Luxembourg Income Survey (June).

Foote Whyte, William. 1993. *Street Corner Society.* 4th ed. University of Chicago Press.

Frey, Bruno and Alois Stutzer. 1999b. "Measuring Preferences by Subjective Well-Being." *Journal of Institutional and Theoretical Economics* 155 (4): 755–78.

———. 2000. "Happiness, Economics, and Institutions." *Economic Journal* 110 (466): 918–38.

Gaddy, Clifford G., and Barry W. Ickes. Forthcoming. *Russia's Virtual Economy.* Brookings.

———. 1998. "Russia's Virtual Economy." *Foreign Affairs* 77 (September/October): 53–68.

Geddes, Barbara. 1995. "The Politics of Economic Liberalization." *Latin American Research Review* 30 (2): 195–214.

Glewwe, Paul, and Gillette Hall. 1998. "Are Some Groups More Vulnerable to Macroeconomic Shocks than Others? Hypothesis Tests Based on Panel Data from Peru." *Journal of Development Economics* 56: 181–206.

Graham, Carol. 1994. *Safety Nets, Politics, and the Poor: Transitions to Market Economies.* Brookings.

———. 1998. *Private Markets for Public Goods: Raising the Stakes in Economic Reform.* Brookings.

———. 2000. "Mobility, Opportunity, and Vulnerability: The Dynamics of Poverty and Inequality in a Global Economy." Background paper prepared for the *Human Development Report 2001.* New York: United Nations Development Programme.

Graham, Carol, and Cheikh Kane. 1998. "Opportunistic Government or Sustaining Reform: Electoral Trends and Public Expenditure Patterns in Peru, 1990–95." *Latin American Research Review* 33 (1): 71–111.

Graham, Carol, and Moises Naím. 1998. "The Political Economy of Institutional Reform in Latin America." In Birdsall, Graham, and Sabot (1998).

Graham, Carol, and Stefano Pettinato. 2000. "Hardship and Happiness: Mobility and Public Perceptions during Market Reforms." *World Economics* 1 (4): 73–112.

———. 2001. "Happiness, Markets, and Democracy: Latin America in Comparative Perspective." *Journal of Happiness Studies* 2 (3): 237–68.

———. Forthcoming. "Frustrated Achievers: Winners, Losers, and Subjective Well-Being in New Market Economies." *Journal of Development Studies.*

Graham, Carol, and others. 1999. *Improving the Odds: Political Strategies for Institutional Reform.* Washington: Inter-American Development Bank.

Granovetter, Mark. 1973. "The Strength of Weak Ties." *American Journal of Sociology* 78 (May): 1360–79.

Greenstein, Robert. 1991. "Relieving Poverty: An Alternative View." *Brookings Review* 9 (Summer): 34–35.

Groot, Wim. 2000. "Adaptation and Scale of Reference Bias in Self Assessments of Quality of Life." *Journal of Health Economics* 19: 403–20.

Gurr, Ted Robert. 1970. *Why Men Rebel.* Princeton University Press.

Haggard, Stephan, and Robert Kaufman. 1995. *The Political Economy of Democratic Transitions.* Princeton University Press.

Haggard, Stephan, and Steven B. Webb. 1994. *Voting for Reform: Democracy, Adjustment, and Political Liberalization.* Oxford University Press.

Herrera, Javier. 1999. "Ajuste Económico, Desigualdad y Movilidad." Instituto Nacional de Estadisticas, Lima, Peru.

Hirschman, Albert O. 1973. "Changing Tolerance for Income Inequality in the Course of Economic Development." *Quarterly Journal of Economics* 87 (November): 544–66.

Hoff, Karla. 1996. "Market Failures and the Distribution of Wealth: A Perspective from the Economics of Information." *Politics and Society* 24 (4): 411–32.

Hojman, David. 2000. "Inequality, Growth, and Political Stability: Can Income Mobility Really Provide the Answers?" In Birdsall and Graham (2000).

Inglehart, Ronald. 1988. "The Renaissance of Political Culture." *American Political Science Review* 82 (December): 1203–30.

Inter-American Development Bank. 1998. *Facing Up to Inequality in Latin America: Report on Economic and Social Progress in Latin America, 1998–99.*

International Finance Corporation. 2000. *Paths out of Poverty: The Role of the Private Enterprise in Developing Countries.* Washington.

ICPSR (Inter-University Consortium for Political and Social Research). *General Social Survey, Cumulative File.* University of Michigan (www.icpsr.umich.com).

Kahneman, Daniel, Ed Diener, and Norbert Schwarz. 1999. *Well-Being: The Foundations of Hedonic Psychology.* Russell Sage Foundation.

Kahneman, Daniel, Ilana Ritov, and David Schkade. 1999. "Economic Preferences or Attitude Expressions? An Analysis of Dollar Responses to Public Issues." *Journal of Risk and Uncertainty* 19: 203–35.

Kahneman, Daniel, and Amos Tversky. 2000. *Choices, Values, and Frames.* Russell Sage Foundation and Cambridge University Press.

Kapteyn, Arie. 2000. "Savings and Reference Groups." Paper presented to MacArthur Network on Inequality and Social Interactions. Brookings, Center on Social and Economic Dynamics (December 1999).

Keely, Louise. 2001. "Why Isn't Growth Making Us Happier? Utility on a Hedonic Treadmill." University of Wisconsin and London School of Economics (January).

Kenny, Charles. 1999. "Does Growth Cause Happiness, or Does Happiness Cause Growth?" *Kyklos* 52 (1): 3–26.

Knack, Stephen, and Philip Keefer. 1997. "Does Social Capital Have an Economic Payoff? A Cross-Country Investigation." *Quarterly Journal of Economics* 112 (November): 1251–88.

Koszegi, Botond. 2000. "Ego, Utility, Overconfidence, and Task Choice." University of California at Berkeley (September).

Krackhardt, David. 1992. "The Strength of Strong Ties: The Importance of Phylos." In *Networks and Organizations: Structure, Form, and Action,* edited by Nitin Nohria and Robert G. Eccles. Harvard Business School Press.

Krugman, Paul. 1992. "The Right, the Rich, and the Facts: Deconstructing the Income Distribution Debate." *American Prospect* 11 (Fall): 19-31.

Lam, David, and Robert F. Schoeni. 1993. "Effects of Family Background on Earnings and Returns to Education in Brazil." *Journal of Political Economy* 101 (4): 710–40.

Leibenstein, Harvey. 1962. "Notes on Welfare Economics and the Theory of Democracy." *Economic Journal* 22 (286): 299–319.

Lindert, Peter. 1996. "What Limits Social Spending?" *Explorations in Economic History* 33 (January): 1–34.

Londoño, Juan Luis, Antonio Spilimbergo, and Miguel Székely. 1997. "Income Distribution, Factor Endowments, and Trade Openness." OCE Working Paper 356. Washington: Inter-American Development Bank (October).

Londoño, Juan Luis, and Miguel Székely. 1997. "Distributional Surprises after a Decade of Reforms: Latin America in the Nineties." Washington: Inter-American Development Bank (March).

Lora, Eduardo, and Juan Luis Londoño. 1998. "Structural Reforms and Equity in Latin America." In Birdsall, Graham, and Sabot (1998), 63–90.

Lowenstein, George, Drazen Prelec, and Roberto Weber. 1999. "What, Me Worry? A Psychological Perspective on the Economics of Retirement." *Behavioral Dimensions of Retirement,* edited by Henry J. Aaron. Brookings and Russell Sage Foundation.

Lustig, Nora, ed. 2001. *Shielding the Poor: Social Protection in the Developing World.* Brookings and the Inter-American Development Bank.

Manski, Charles. 1990. "The Use of Intentions Data to Predict Behavior: A Best Case Analysis." *Journal of the American Statistical Association* 85: 934–40.

Marshall, Gordon, and David Firth. 1999. "Social Mobility and Personal Satisfaction: Evidence from Ten Countries." *British Journal of Sociology* 50 (March): 28–48.

Mateju, Petr. 2000. "Mobility and Perceived Change in Life Chances in Post-Communist Countries." In Birdsall and Graham (2000), 291–324.

McFadden, Daniel. Forthcoming. "Rationality for Economists?" *Journal of Risk and Uncertainty* (Special Issue on Preference Elicitation).

McMurrer, Daniel, and Isabel Sawhill, 1998. *Getting Ahead: Economic and Social Mobility in America.* Washington: Urban Institute Press.

Merton, Robert K. 1957. *Social Theory and Social Structure*. Glencoe, Ill.: Free Press of Glencoe.

Michalos, Alex. C. 1980. "Satisfaction and Happiness." *Social Indicators Research* 8: 385–422.

Milanovic, Branko. 1998. *Income, Inequality, and Poverty during the Transition from Planned to Market Economy*. Washington: World Bank.

Milanovic, Branko, and Branko Jovanovic. 1999. "Change in the Perceptions of the Poverty Line during the Times of Depression: Russia, 1993–1996." *World Bank Economic Review* 13 (September): 531–60.

Mishel, Lawrence, Jared Bernstein, and John Schmitt. 1999. *The State of Working America 1998–99*. Cornell University Press.

Morley, Samuel. 1994. *Poverty and Inequality in Latin America*. Johns Hopkins University Press.

Morley, Samuel, Roberto Machado, and Stefano Pettinato. 1999. "Indexes of Structural Reform in Latin America." *Serie Reformas Económicas de la CEPAL*, LC/L.1166. Santiago (January).

Moulton, Brent R. 1990. "An Illustration of a Pitfall in Estimating the Effects of Aggregate Variables on Micro Units." *Review of Economics and Statistics* 72 (2): 334–38.

Namazie, Ceema, and Peter Sanfey. 1998. "Happiness in Transition: The Case of Kyrgyzstan." Discussion Paper 40. London School of Economics, Distributional Analysis Research Programme (July).

Nelson, Joan M. 1976. *Access to Power*. Harvard University Press.

Nike, Inc. 1998. *Annual Report to the Securities and Exchange Commission* (8/29).

Okun, Arthur. 1975. *Equality and Efficiency, The Big Tradeoff*. Brookings.

Oswald, Andrew. 1997. "Happiness and Economic Performance." *Economic Journal* 107 (November): 4–45.

Pastor, Manuel, and Carol Wise. 1999. "The Politics of Second Generation Reforms." *Journal of Democracy* 10: 34–48.

Pastore, José, and Nelson do Valle Silva. 2000. *Mobilidade Social no Brasil*. Sao Paulo: Makron Books.

Perlman, Janice. 1976. *The Myth of Marginality*. University of California Press.

———. 1999. "Method Notes and Exploratory Interviews for Repeat Study of Rio Favelas." Document presented at the World Bank (September). Details on progress of study are available at www.megacities.trincoll.edu.

Pettinato, Stefano. 2000. "A Conceptual Primer to Inequality." Background paper prepared for the *Human Development Report 2001*. New York: United Nations Development Programme (October).

Pettinato, Stefano, Ross Hammond, and Carol Graham. Forthcoming. "What Drives the Frustrations of the Achievers? A Satisfaction Model with Consumption Vision and Status Awareness." Working Paper. Brookings, Center on Social and Economic Dynamics.

Pigou, A. C. 1920. *The Economics of Welfare*. Macmillan.

Piketty, Thomas. 1995. "Social Mobility and Redistributive Politics." *Quarterly Journal of Economics* 110 (August): 551–84.

Pritchett, Lant, and Jonathan Gelbard. 1997. "More for the Poor Is Less for the Poor: The Politics of Targeting." Policy Research Working Paper 1799. Washington: World Bank (July).

Pritchett, Lant, Asep Suryahadi, and Sudarno Sumarto. 2000. "Quantifying Vulnerability to Poverty: A Proposed Measure with Application to Indonesia." Washington: World Bank (January).

Przeworski, Adam. 1991. *Democracy and the Market.* Cambridge University Press.

Putnam, Robert. 1993. *Making Democracy Work: Civic Traditions in Modern Italy.* Princeton University Press.

Ravallion, Martin, and Michael Loshkin. 1999a. "Subjective Economic Welfare." Policy Research Working Paper 2106. Washington: World Bank (April).

———. 1999b. "Who Wants to Redistribute? Russia's Tunnel Effect in the 1990s." Policy Research Working Paper 2150. Washington: World Bank (July).

Rawls, John. 1971. *A Theory of Justice.* Cambridge, Mass.: Belknap Press.

Richardson, Lewis F. 1960. *Statistics of Deadly Quarrels.* Pittsburgh: Boxwood Press.

Robbins, Donald. 1996. "HOS Hits Facts: Facts Win. Evidence on Trade and Wage Inequality in the Developing World." Development Discussion Paper 557. Harvard Institute for International Development (October).

Robson, Arthur J. 1992. "Status, the Distribution of Wealth, Private and Social Attitudes towards Risk." *Econometrica* 60 (July): 837–57.

Rodrik, Dani. 1996. "Understanding Economic Policy Reform." *Journal of Economic Literature* 34 (March): 9–41.

———. 1999. "Why Is There so Much Insecurity in Latin America?" Harvard University, Kennedy School of Government (October).

Rose, Richard, and A. McAllister. 1996. "Is Money the Measure of Welfare in Russia?" *Review of Income and Wealth* 42 (March): 75–90.

Russia Longitudinal Monitoring Survey. Surveys from 1995 and 1998–99. Carolina Population Center. University of North Carolina (www.cpc.unc.edu/projects/rlms/rlms_home.html).

Rutkowski, Jan. J. 1999. "Earnings Mobility during the Transition. The Case of Hungary, 1992–1997." Washington: World Bank, Europe and Central Asia Department (June).

Saavedra, Jaime. 1998. *Empleo, Productividad e Ingresos en Peru (1990–1996).* International Labor Organization, Lima, Peru.

Sachs, Jeffrey, and Andrew Warner. 1995. "Economic Reform and the Process of Global Integration." *Brookings Papers on Economic Activity* 1: 1–96.

Sawhill, Isabel. "Opportunity in the United States: Myth or Reality?" In Birdsall and Graham (2000).

Schor, Juliet. 1998. *The Overspent American: Upscaling, Downshifting, and the New Consumer.* Basic Books.

Seligson, Amber. 1999. "Civic Association and Democratic Participation in Central America: A Test of the Putnam Thesis." *Comparative Political Studies* 32 (May): 342–62.

Sen, Amartya. 1983. "Poor, Relatively Speaking." *Oxford Economic Papers* 35: 153–69.

———. 1995. "The Political Economy of Targeting." *Public Spending and the Poor: Theory and Evidence*, edited by Dominique Van de Walle and Kimberly Nead, 11–24. Johns Hopkins University Press for the World Bank.

Sheahan, John, and Enrique Iglesias. 1998. "Kinds and Causes of Inequality in Latin America." In Birdsall, Graham, and Sabot (1998).

Shome, P. 1999. "Taxation in Latin America: Structural Trends and Impact of Administration." In XI Seminario Regional de Politica Fiscal. CEPAL. Brasília.

Simon, Herbert. 1978. "Rationality as a Process and Product of Thought." *American Economic Review* 68 (May, *Papers and Proceedings*): 1–16.

Skocpol, Theda. 1991. "Universal Appeal: Politically Viable Policies to Combat Poverty." *Brookings Review* 9 (Summer): 28–33.

Solon, Gary. 1992. "Intergenerational Mobility in the United States." *American Economic Review* 82 (3): 393–408.

Stiglitz, Joseph E. 2000. "Reflections on Mobility and Social Justice, Economic Efficiency, and Individual Responsibility." In Birdsall and Graham (2000).

Stokes, Susan. 1996. "Public Opinion and Market Reforms: The Limits of Economic Voting." *Comparative Political Studies* 29 (October): 499–519.

Székely, Miguel, and Marianne Hilgert. 1999. "What's Behind the Inequality We Measure? An Investigation Using Latin American Data for the 1990s." Washington: Inter-American Development Bank.

Tanzi, Vito. 2000. "Globalization and the Future of Social Protection." Working Paper. Washington: International Monetary Fund (January).

Tanzi, Vito, and Howell H. Zee. 2000. "Tax Policy for Emerging Markets— Developing Countries." Working Paper. Washington: International Monetary Fund (March).

Terrell, Katherine. 2000. "Worker Mobility and Transition to a Market Economy: Winners and Losers." In Birdsall and Graham (2000).

Thaler, Richard. 2000. "From Homo Economicus to Homo Sapiens." *Journal of Economic Perspectives* 14 (Winter): 133–42.

United Nations Development Programme. 1998. *Human Development Report 1998.* New York.

Van de Walle, Dominique, and Kimberly Nead, eds. 1995. *Public Spending and the Poor: Theory and Evidence.* Johns Hopkins University Press for the World Bank.

Van Praag, Bernard M. S., and Paul Frijters. 1999. "The Measurement of Welfare and Well-Being: The Leyden Approach." In Kahneman, Diener, and Schwarz (1999).

Veblen, Thorstein. 1967. *The Theory of the Leisure Class.* Penguin.

Vecernik, Jiri. 1996. *Markets and People: The Czech Reform Explained in Comparative Perspective.* Aldershot, U.K.: Avebury Press.

Veenhoven, Ruut. 1991. "Is Happiness Relative?" *Social Indicators Research* 24: 1–34.

Webb, Richard. 2000. "Household Perceptions of Mobility in a New Market Economy: Peru 1998." In Birdsall and Graham (2000), 267–90.

Weyland, Kurt. 1998. "Peasants or Bankers in Venezuela? Presidential Popularity and Economic Reform Approval, 1989–1993." *Political Research Quarterly* 51 (June): 341–62.

Wolfson, Michael C. 1997. "Divergent Inequalities: Theory and Empirical Results." Research Paper Series 6. Ottawa: Statistics Canada, Analytical Studies Branch.

World Bank. 1999. *Poverty and Social Developments in Peru, 1994–1997.* Washington.

———. 2000. *World Development Report: Attacking Poverty.* Washington.

Yaqub, Shahin. 2000. "Born Poor, Stay Poor? The Intergenerational Persistence of Poverty." Background paper for the *Human Development Report, 2001.* New York: United Nations Development Programme (September).

Young, Peyton. 1994. *Equity: Principles and Practice.* Princeton University Press.

———. 1999. "Diffusion in Social Networks." Working Paper 2. Brookings, Center on Social and Economic Dynamics (June).

Index

Age: and economic satisfaction, 116; effects on support for redistribution, 93, 132; effects on views of income, 27; and happiness, 76, 94, 116–17, 130, 140–41; and job satisfaction, 117; perceived past mobility and, 110, 115, 116, 128–30; perceptions gaps and, 124; subjective evaluations, 27–28
Alesina, Alberto, 29, 30–31
Argentina: inequality and redistribution, 84
Asia: growth and savings, 52–53
Australia: happiness studies, 28, 80

Behavioral economics, 3, 5, 16–17, 151
Behrman, Jere R., 48–49
Benabou, Roland, 2, 96–97
Bentham, Jeremy, 16
Birdsall, Nancy, 10, 48–49, 52–53, 61–62, 65
Biswas-Diener, Robert, 23, 28–29
Blanchflower, David G., 15, 25
Bolivia: tolerance of inequality, 84

Brazil: education spending, 59; income mobility, 58; relationship of education and income, 51, 52, 55–56, 58
Britain: effects of mobility, 31; factors in happiness, 25, 80, 87; reference norms for health status, 28

Capital markets, 6. *See also* Economic integration, international
Central America: community organizations, 34; tolerance of inequality, 84. *See also* Costa Rica; El Salvador; Latin America
Children: parental expectations, 117. *See also* Education
Chile: happiness levels, 85; income inequality, 49–50, 84; market reforms, 81; poverty, 49; social expenditures, 59; support for market reforms, 82, 84
China: income mobility, 42
Cities. *See* Urban areas
Clark, Andrew E., 24
Class. *See* Social class

167